Celtic Gods, Celtic Goddesses

CELTIC GODS
CELTIC GODDESSES

R.J. STEUART

ILLUSTRATED BY

MIRANDA GRAY

AND

COURTNEY DAVIS

BLANDFORD

Blandford
An imprint of Cassell
Villiers House, 41/47 Strand, London WC2N 5JE

First published 1990
Reprinted 1991
First published in paperback 1992
Reprinted 1992

Distributed in the United States by
Sterling Publishing Co. Inc.
387 Park Avenue, New York, NY 10016-8810

Distributed in Australia by
Capricorn Link (Australia) Pty Ltd
PO Box 665, Lane Grove, NSW 2066

British Library Cataloguing in Publication Data

Stewart, R. J. (Robert J), *1949–*
   Celtic gods, Celtic goddesses.
   1. Europe. Celts. Religious life, ancient period
   I. Title
   299'.16

ISBN 0-7137-2108-1 hardback
ISBN 0-7137-2113-8

Typeset by Asco Trade Typesetting Ltd, Hong Kong
Printed and bound in Hong Kong by
Colorcraft Ltd

Contents

THE COLOUR ILLUSTRATIONS
page 7

ACKNOWLEDGEMENTS
page 8

FOREWORD
page 9

INTRODUCTION
page 19

THE CELTS
page 25

THE CELTS AND NATURE
page 37

TOTEM ANIMALS
page 48

MOTHER GODDESSES
page 58

CELTIC GODDESSES
page 64

BRIGHID/MINERVA
page 93

THE DIVINE ANCESTOR AND THE SON OF LIGHT
page 102

THE CELTIC GODS
page 114

INVASIONS, MANIFESTATIONS, DIVISIONS
page 126

AFTERWORD
page 139

APPENDIX: MATH, SON OF MATHONWY
page 141

NOTES ON FURTHER READING
page 155

INDEX OF NAMES AND PLACES
page 157

GENERAL INDEX
page 159

The Colour Illustrations

The images of Celtic gods and goddesses chosen for this book are arranged in a seasonal and cyclical order. They are not intended as a complete or detailed pantheon, and there are a number of alternative ways of showing the cycle, which begins and ends at midwinter midnight. For the Celtic names and functions of each god or goddess, see individual captions with each colour illustration.

1 **The Lord of Light**   Destroys Chaos.

2 **The Flower Maiden**   Goddess of flowering transient beauty. Spring/dawn.

3 **The Lord of the Animals**   God of herds, forests and the forces of life and death in nature. Spring/dawn.

4 **Lady of Bright Inspiration**   Goddess of light, poetry and therapy. Spring/midday.

5 **The Young Son of Light**   God of liberation and music. Early summer/midday.

6 **The Hero**   Son of the Lord of Light, protector of the land. Midsummer/midday.

7 **The Lord of Thunder**   Bringer of energetic transformation. Late summer/afternoon.

8 **Queen of Horses and Fruitfulness**   Autumn/evening.

9 **Phantom Queen of Death, Sexuality and Conflict**   Winter/night.

10 **The Sea God**   Navigator of the stars and oceans. Midwinter/midnight.

Acknowledgements

I would like to acknowledge Bath City Council Museum Service for permission to photograph the Romano–Celtic carvings associated with the temple complex and Temple of Sulis Minerva, which is conveniently located adjacent to and beneath my house. General acknowledgement must be made to a host of translators, archaeologists, interpreters, poets, visionaries, bards and writers, including, but by no means limited to, the work of:

Ann Ross
Barry Cunliffe
Caitlín Matthews
Edward Davis
Frederick Bligh Bond (from his private notes)
Geoffrey of Monmouth
J. A. Giles
Lady Charlotte Guest
Proinsias MacCana
Robert Graves
Robert Kirk
William Sharp (Fiona Macleod)
J. J. Parry

Specific acknowledgement must be made to W. G. Gray, who introduced me to the ritual complex of the Rollright Stones about twenty years ago, thereby opening doors into the world of legend and mythology, and into the Sacred Land that lives beyond but close to our own.

Foreword

Preparing a short book on a vast subject is like a riddle or paradoxical task found in Celtic legend: 'Summarize the creation of the universe and all its beings in a few pages, and illustrate them for the reader!' Fortunately much of the work has already been done by Celtic masters of poetry and story telling, ranging from anonymous bards to monastic chroniclers and the medieval works of Geoffrey of Monmouth. The addition of modern archaeological evidence gives factual credence to oral tradition and legendary inspired truth, and these streams of evidence should be set in a healthy balance with one another.

I have not followed the customary modern route of separating Welsh, Irish and Scots, and Romano–British and Gaulish material, that is found in many of the detailed major studies. This book is based instead upon the primal functions of Celtic mythology and magic, which are as follows:

1 The **People**
2 The **Mother Goddesses**
3 The **Father Gods**
4 The **Son** and **Daughter** divinities
5 The **Heroes**
6 The **Kingship** and the **Sovereign Land**
7 **Magical Cosmology**

These seven fundamental aspects of Celtic religion and culture are impossible to separate artificially, though I have dedicated chapters to certain general headings, as may be seen from the list of contents. As this is a non-academic book, I have reserved the freedom of following the gods and goddesses intuitively and poetically, though the path taken is always well sign-posted with evidence from classical Celtic and medieval literature, folklore, archaeology and (to a lesser extent) comparative religion.

The images and concepts, therefore, cross over frequently between sources in Welsh and Irish legend, Romano–Celtic archaeology and literature, even relatively 'modern' sources of folk tradition that clearly preserve ancient ceremonial patterns and beliefs. I would like to declare and emphasize at this point that there is no firm suggestion in this book of a formal unity or pantheon to Celtic gods and goddesses. The reasons for this are dealt with in the relevant chapters, but I would not wish to be accused of (or even blessed for) generating a unified vision of Celtic mythology, particularly as I believe that the great wonder and strength of Celtic magic is that it has no rigid boundaries or self-styled 'complete systems'.

The cyclical nature of Celtic religion, from darkness to light to darkness, is the only firm pattern on which this book is founded. The other patterns and relationships of the gods and goddesses, magic and cosmology, which appear plentifully, are examples or selections to demonstrate how such imaginative material endures in Celtic culture, from pre-Roman times to the present day.

AIMS AND USES OF THIS BOOK

Celtic Gods, Celtic Goddesses offers insights into Celtic mythology. It is not primarily an archaeological or linguistic study, though detailed evidence is drawn from many such sources, but aims to define and relate the gods and goddesses of the ancient Celts as living forces in the imagination and worship of the widespread Celtic people. Such imaginative forces are closely linked to the land and deepest spiritual impulses of humankind worldwide, and are by no means limited to the Celts or any other cultural group. Each region or land, however, generates its own unique imagery; the beliefs of the ancient Celts persist even into the present day in European and Western tradition, often in curious and surprising forms, diffused worldwide by the migrations of people.

Most books on Celtic religion are detailed academic works, aimed at the scholar and long-term student. The subject is vast, and continually develops, clarifying as new research and interpretation appears, ranging through archaeology, literature, epigraphy and iconography. More recently there has been a growing move towards a psychological interpretation of ancient religions, though this may be fraught with the danger of over-reductionism.

There are very few books, however, that give us an overview, an insight into Celtic religion, magic and mythology, and organize that overview into an accessible format for direct use, either by the academic or non-academic reader. *Celtic Gods, Celtic Goddesses* aims to provide such an overview, showing how the gods and goddesses that occur in such complexity and profusion in Celtic sources may indeed have related to one another and to the beliefs, worship and magical practices of the people themselves. In an age when environmental concerns are increasingly important, even essential to basic survival, the patterns and imagery of the ancient Celtic religion, so intimately involved with the health of the land, are particularly resonant and appealing to the modern imagination.

THE REDISCOVERY OF CELTIC MYTH AND MAGIC

When Celtic legends were rediscovered by Victorian scholars, and later confirmed in many ways by modern archaeology, the gods and goddesses of the Celts were regarded as quaint, barbaric and often incomprehensible. This attitude persists even today in many books, and the detailed nature of major academic works tends to reinforce, unintentionally, an illusion of unapproachable complexity and obscurity within Celtic myth, religion and magical or philosophical belief. This illusion is further reinforced by certain major differences of attitude between ourselves and the ancient Celts: we tend to assume that they followed, at the least, logical lines of thought similar to those found within the Roman culture that conquered Celtic Europe. We even demand that the ancient Celts think like modern Westerners. Much of our confusion over Celtic

Relief of Esus (*c*. first century BC) from Trier.

culture and mythology comes from such unacknowledged demands, heavily tinged by our orthodox political–religious background of monotheism.

This book aims to demonstrate the nature of Celtic deities and reveal the beautiful and often profound beliefs and philosophy that underpin the characters and legends. The Celts held goddesses, and magical or transcendent feminine powers, in particular reverence, and Celtic mythology demonstrates a deep understanding of both nature and the human psyche in the way gods, goddesses, heroes and mortals relate to one another.

The foundation of Celtic religion is the sacred quality of the land, symbolized by a potent Goddess of Sovereignty. From this primal figure, who is often associated with love, death and sexuality, all other mythical figures derive. The great Heroes, often found with solar and Underworld attributes, are her sons; the culture goddesses, who assist, enable and sometimes transform human development, are her daughters. Within this broad framework our heritage of Celtic myth, legend, folklore, and its supportive archaeological evidence, is coherent and meaningful.

There is a further level of meaning and origin to Celtic gods and goddesses, which has seldom been discussed or analysed. Beyond the goddesses of the land and their associated sons and daughters there are stellar or cosmic figures described in Celtic legend. These are often deeper aspects of environmental or heroic characters. The Welsh goddess Arianrhod, a character in the medieval story collection *The Mabinogion*[1] but clearly deriving from pre-Christian tradition, whose name means 'Silver Wheel', is not only a local or national deity preserved in myth and legend, but is a stellar figure, associated with observation of a group of stars. She is related in many ways to the Greek Ariadne, the goddess of the maze and thread, who also has a stellar significance.

The obscure *Prophecies of Merlin*[2], set out from Celtic bardic tradition in the twelfth century by Geoffrey of Monmouth, include a powerful apocalyptic astrological vision, in which a goddess called Ariadne unravels the solar system. Such thresholds of early literature, preserving traditions and mythic patterns that were originally oral, can give us many insights into Celtic religion, cosmology, worship and magical arts. Many great kings and heroes in famous legends, such as Bran the Blessed, or even King Arthur, have connections to a primal and enduring mythology involving the constellations.

Celtic legends may be broadly defined as working on three levels:

The first is that of adventure, as heroic comic and tragic tales preserved in early literature, oral tradition and folk tales and ballads. Upon this level we find a panoply of characters such as Arthur, Arianrhod, Cuchulainn, the Green Knight, Bran the Blessed, Brighid, the Morrigan, people larger than life but still with many human characteristics. This traditional corpus, found in both literature and oral entertainment and education, cannot be too strongly emphasized as a source for comparison with archaeological and other evidence from the ancient world.

The second is that of sanctity of the land, in which the characters first encountered in tales as heroic or dramatic personae are revealed as pagan gods and goddesses connected to the welfare of both environment and clan or tribe. This second level merges gradually with Celtic Christianity, giving rise to the

11

astonishing Grail legends, which are a major expression of Celtic magic, tradition and metaphysics.

The third level relates to the stars, and shows gods and goddesses of the environment, of nature, to be reflections or localized versions of stellar or cosmic figures. On this level they have a role which is echoed worldwide in myth, religion, magic and ancient traditions. The giant king Bran, for example, is not only a British guardian of the land, but closely related in concept, nature, and perhaps historic tradition, to the Greek Titan Cronos, ruler of a Golden Age and magical island[3]. Bran also represents, on the formidable side of his nature, the constellation of Orion, which was of major importance to sailors, traders, and farmers in early cultures. Orion was seen as a giant, heaving his broad shoulders over the horizon to herald the time of storms and winter weather.

> Bendigeid Vran, with the host of which we spoke, sailed towards Ireland, and was not far across the sea when he came to shoal water. . . . Then he proceeded with what provisions he had on his own back, and approached the shore of Ireland.
>
> Now the swineherds of Matholwch were upon the sea shore, and they came to Matholwch. 'Lord,' said they, 'greeting be unto thee.' 'And Heaven protect you,' replied he, 'Have you any news?' 'Lord,' said they, 'we bring marvellous news, for we have seen a wood upon the sea, in a place where we never yet saw a single tree!' 'This is indeed a marvel,' said he; 'and saw you anything else?' 'We saw, lord,' said they, 'a vast mountain beside the wood, which moved, and there was a lofty ridge on the top of the mountain, and a lake on each side of the ridge. And the wood, and the mountain, and all these things moved together.' 'Verily' said Matholwch, 'there is none who can know aught concerning this, unless it be Branwen.'
>
> So messengers were sent to Branwen. 'Lady' said they, 'what thinkest thou this is?' 'The men of the Island of the Mighty [Britain], who have come hither on hearing of my ill treatment and my woes.' 'What is this forest that is seen upon the sea?' asked the messengers. 'The masts and yards of ships,' she replied. 'Alas,' said they, 'and what is the mountain that is seen by the side of the ships?' 'That is Bendigeid Vran, my brother,' she replied, 'coming to shoal water; there is no ship that can contain him within itself.' 'And what,' asked the messenger, 'is the lofty ridge with a lake on each side thereof?' 'On looking towards this land of Ireland he is wroth, and his two eyes, one on each side of his nose, are the two lakes beside the ridge.'
>
> (From 'Branwen the Daughter of Llyr', *The Mabinogion*, translated by Lady Charlotte Guest)

Many Celtic myths, tales and customs relate to mysterious legends such as those of the Pleiades, a small star group used worldwide (in both northern and southern hemispheres) to mark the turning points of spring and winter, established through observation. Even today genuine traditional dance dramas are found in Europe which celebrate death and resurrection at the setting of the Pleiades in May. One such ceremony, the Padstow Hobby Horse, in the west of England, has all the hallmarks of a pagan ritual of considerable antiquity, even in its amended twentieth-century form. Furthermore we know from earlier records of the Padstow ceremony that many of the elements of Celtic religion were present, though the sequence has been changed since the turn of the century and certain parts of the ceremony abandoned[4].

The power of Celtic gods has survived in such ceremonies right into the age of computers and television. It has also survived and been regenerated in a vast

Silvered torc from Trichtingen, Württemberg.

body of story-telling, literature, film, television and popular belief. Although they may be disguised in many ways, the Celtic gods and goddesses are by no means extinct within our imagination.

The following chapters outline pagan and early Christian Celtic culture and examine a selection of Celtic gods and goddesses from Britain, Ireland and Europe, covering most of the 'major' figures. But certain apparently 'minor' figures are also described, for there is no hard and fast hierarchy of Celtic gods and goddesses, and much of the significant evidence is in the form of allusions, asides, single images or references.

IMAGES OF CELTIC DEITIES

There are many problems associated with the imagery of gods and goddesses, and Celtic deities are more problematical than most in this respect. During the nineteenth century it was often assumed, because people apparently worshipped images of animals or of theriomorphic creatures combining human and animal attributes, that they thought such animals were indeed gods and goddesses. This inaccurate viewpoint is partly the unfortunate result of orthodox dogma, in which all 'other' religions are regarded with jealous scorn, and it is further complicated by the arrogance of modern science, psychology and materialism, whereby it is automatically assumed that all matters from past cultures have been superseded, or may be rationally labelled and explained.

The images of Celtic gods and goddesses that remain to us for study are almost entirely from the period of the Roman invasions of Gaul and Britain; they are heavily influenced by classical symbolism, though often retaining a uniquely Celtic quality, and certainly uphold many specific attributes of the native Celtic gods and goddesses despite classical parallels and fusions. It seems unlikely that the pre-Roman Celts made extensive images of their deities, and they did not employ direct representation in their native art, which tended towards stylism and traditional patterns rather than natural imagery. What little we know of Celtic art corresponds to the reports of classical historians and to the evidence of later Celtic tradition; the Celtic culture was primarily held together by oral traditions of great sophistication and complexity. Concrete images such as statues or pictures, therefore, were not employed, for it was through poetic imagery in verse, song, or declamation and story-telling, that divine or magical images were communicated and preserved.

Celtic shrines and temples probably did not contain statues of deities until after the Roman invasions and conquests; in Ireland it is quite clear that the sacred groves and stones of the Druids were, in themselves, devoid of image. Thus a *nemed* or sacred grove might contain living or dead trees, a sacred spring, and perhaps a stone altar or upright standing stone, possibly inherited from the pre-Celtic religion.

It seems likely that the Celts used the megalithic worship sites which cover western Europe, though we have little detailed evidence for such use other than archaeological finds; thus we know that use was made of such sites, but not what

---

FIGURE A THE FIVEFOLD PATTERN, OR WHEEL OF BEING

The Pattern consists of four Zones or Directions, unified by a fifth; it may be shown as five rings, as in our example, or more simply as a circle divided equally into four quarters (1 + 4 = 5). As a conceptual model it has appeared repeatedly from ancient times, and is still employed today, in various presentations, in traditional magical arts worldwide. It is the basis for many of the typical patterns found in Celtic geometric art, and for a number of philosophical or metaphysical maps and glyphs; in spherical form it provides the ground plan for the Platonic Solids, a series of mathematical topological forms which define dimensions and conditions of universal existence. Ancient Ireland was symbolically divided into four Provinces, with a unifying or central fifth; the pattern of the bardic or Druidic universe, presented in the medieval *Vita Merlini* drawn from Celtic and classical traditions, was likewise one of Four Powers or Elements, unified by a Fifth Principle of Balance. This was reflected in the *Vita* by the pattern of the planet Earth, divided into Four Zones with a temperate Fifth in which the Land of Britain was located. It seems very likely that England, Wales and Scotland were each similarly patterned, with certain potent locations marking the four directions and the centre. Greater Britain itself, of course, comprises the four individual lands of Ireland, Scotland, Wales and England, divisions which have survived in various forms since the earliest known records of the land ... with the once separate land of Cornwall making a fifth. We have no indication from tradition, however, if the five lands of Britain were ever considered to be harmonically related in the manner of the five Provinces of Ireland, though the analogy is tempting.

KEY TO FIGURE A

The Four Powers, Directions, Elements and Seasons
1 Life/East/Air/Spring/Dawn
2 Light/South/Fire/Summer/Noon
3 Love/West/Water/Autumn/Evening
4 Law/North/Earth/Winter/Night

The Four Implements of Power in Ancient Irish Tradition
1 The Sword of Nuadha (or Arrow)
2 The Spear of Lugh (or Rod)
3 The Cauldron of the Daghdha (or Cup)
4 The Stone of Fal (or Shield or Mirror)

In magical traditions the Sword, Rod, Cup and Shield are unified by the Cord, while the Four Elements are unified by Spirit.

The Provinces and Potencies of Ancient Ireland
1 East (Leinster): BENEFIT, *Farmers or householders*, prosperity, hospitality.
3 South (Munster): MUSIC, *Poets and minstrels*, knowledge, fertility.
3 West (Connaught): LEARNING, *Druids*, judgment, chronicles, story-telling.
4 North (Ulster): BATTLE, *Warriors*, conflict, struggle, pride.
5 Centre (Meath): KINGSHIP, *The King and Stewards*, stability, bounty, renown.

form that use took or how significant the sites were to the Celts. There are, however, a number of traditions concerning the mysterious Underworld or Otherworld, and this is frequently associated in folklore or early literature with megalithic sites in addition to natural features such as hills, springs or caves. In Ireland, for example, the gods and goddesses were allocated certain specific *sidh* or ancient mounds, and these allocations remained in popular lore well into the twentieth century[5].

Celtic religion was primarily associated with the sanctity of the land, and the power of certain key locations within the land. The entire landscape or environment was alive ... the sacred groves or shrines were places of special power within an indivisible entity, a continuum. The land was usually represented by a goddess, whose shape was clear to see in the rise of the hills and whose powers were apparent in the flow of rivers, the rising of springs and the growth of plants. This does *not*, however, suggest that the Celts were mere 'nature worshippers' and that they bowed down to trees and stones; they had a whole vision of the sanctity of life and land, unified and harmonized together. The entire range of Celtic tradition is, in fact, filled with patterns of harmony, unity, and the direction or attuning of the land and its people. In Ireland the sacred divisions of the land, the Four Directions, the model of kingship and the royal

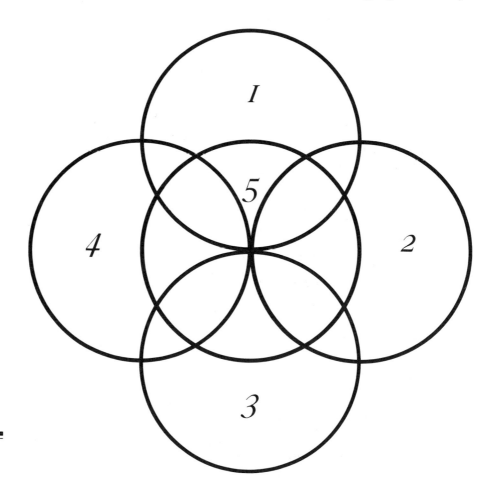

The Four Directions and
Five Zones

15

court, were all firmly based upon an organic and sacro-magical system of patterns[6]. When the pattern was right, all went well; when the pattern was disturbed, ills arose.

The 'decorative' quality so often commented upon in true Celtic art, found in both early pre-Roman influence and late Dark Age or even medieval works, is directly connected to the Celtic concept of patterns of energy. If we wish to understand how the Celts saw their world, we need to sit and contemplate such patterns. They are not decorations at all, in the modern sense, but statements of a vision of reality[7].

How, therefore, do direct images of gods and goddesses fit into this inter-woven world of patterns and energies? This difficult question may, perhaps, be approached by stepping back in time and considering those images known to us from Romano–Celtic temples. They were attempts to formalize traditions of worship that had been virtually, but not entirely, formless until the Roman conquests. The new state politics imposed upon the Celts demanded formal statements of deities, and these had to be integrated with those of Rome for direct purposes of authority. Thus curious hybrid images arose, attempts to satisfy Celt and Roman or Romanized mercenary alike.

The modern student of Celtic tradition, however, has a quite different prob-lem; we are so accustomed to exteriorized images, particularly in the context of widespread television, that we find it hard to grasp Celtic deities without them. There needs to be, therefore, an attempt at redefining the images in a relatively 'pure' form, even though such forms were never employed by the pre-Roman Celts themselves. In other words, we need to restore the pictures of the gods and goddesses by sifting through all the available evidence, and then using our imagination with both inspiration and caution. Fortunately there is a mass of material from early literature and folklore that helps us to redefine such images and compare them with Romanized variants from Britain and Gaul.

THE COLOUR ILLUSTRATIONS

The colour illustrations in this book are not offered as firm or authoritative

Bull carved in stone from Burghead, Morayshire, Scotland.

16

statements of what the Celts saw as their gods and goddesses; they are carefully researched versions of the major images and attributes, presented for the modern reader. Some Romanized influences have been removed, wherever detected, and certain themes or symbols from Celtic literature have been included. The colour illustrations are therefore a fusion of archaeological evidence, literary evidence, and tradition. They are included to help us see the Celtic gods and goddesses in an un-Romanized and, perhaps more important, unromanticized form. There has been a constant tendency in art from the nineteenth century to the present day to show Celtic deities as wan, ethereal or even comic-strip characters; such images derive from quite modern literary works rather than Celtic tradition.

THE LINE DRAWINGS

The line drawings are based directly upon archaeological evidence, drawn from specific photographs of carefully researched and documented remains. In a few cases a tentative restoration has been made, to help the reader see how the original might have looked before time or conflict took toll upon the original work, but no attempt has been made to 'improve' or unify the fragments. Some of the line drawings show those typically Celtic patterns, dating from the earliest pre-Roman period to the monastic manuscripts of the Celtic Christian Church. While the colour illustrations are modern imaginative restatements based upon extensive evidence from many sources, the line drawings represent some of the sources of evidence in as accurate a representation as possible.

The Three Mothers.
Romano–Celtic relief from
Vertillum, Burgundy.

17

THE PHOTOGRAPHS

The photographs have been chosen to give some indication of two major sources for evidence of Celtic religion: natural sites and artifacts found upon the sites. The literary and traditional evidence is covered by the examples in each chapter of our text.

As the sanctity of the land was central to Celtic religion, some of our photographs show a selection of sacred sites in Britain dating back to prehistoric times, many of which still have traditions of magic attached to them today. Other photographs show Romano–Celtic relief carving or statuary; most of our examples in this category are from the extensive temple complex of Aquae Sulis[8] in Bath in the west of England in which classical and Celtic religion fused together around the focus of sacred springs. The temple complex of Aquae Sulis is a particularly good example of the fusion of Roman and Celtic cultures, and demonstrates the reverence for water sources, with its ample hot springs. The site also has many typical traditions of pagan religion and mythology, some of which were still asserted in medieval literature centuries after the physical remains of the temple itself were buried beneath the later accumulations of mud and, of course, beneath the ever-growing city.

The illustrations, ranging from factual to imaginative, cover the wide area of places, styles, objects, and descriptions or visions relating to Celtic gods and goddesses. Ultimately we encounter the deities in our visions, in dreams, or more rarely in moments of inspiration in sacred places. Such poetic truths are as real and potent for us today as they were for our ancestors.

R. J. Stewart, Bath

Introduction

There have been many changes in our attitude to ancient gods and goddesses in the last hundred years: until the nineteenth century they were almost entirely considered to be aspects of a classical scholar's Greek or Roman education, fit for poets but not for worship. Three hundred years or so earlier, the Renaissance revived a flood of classical Greek and Roman pagan material but, apart from very specific and often secret esoteric traditions or magical arts, this was generally assembled within an overall Christian context and a Christian orthodox society. Many of the confused modern attitudes to classical pagan mythology may be traced back to the enthusiasm and vivid imagery of Renaissance artists and writers.

Even when the repressive straitjacket of decayed Christianity was unfastened in the twentieth century, ancient Celtic gods and goddesses were still considered to be 'variants' of the classical pantheon. Today we have an extreme swing in the opposite direction, in which modern neo-pagans claim to worship and establish satisfactory relationships with ancient god and goddess forms; this revolution is particularly strong in its emphasis of the feminine powers, those of goddesses or the Goddess.

How effective such paganism may be in improving our lives or in changing modern society constructively is impossible to estimate at present, but it seems likely that modern revivals often shoot wide of the mark when they aim at restoring ancient forms and techniques of worship. In this context we should obviously exclude the more absurd lunatic elements, and consider only serious and, hopefully, well-researched efforts at offering alternative forms of worship, wonder and fruit for the imagination in a materialist culture.

Increasing understanding of Celtic tradition began through nineteenth-century reappraisal of Celtic literature, a powerful movement which led to a parallel understanding in modern archaeology. Today Celtic gods and goddesses are accepted by academic authorities as true and complex entities, rather than obscure curiosities vaguely related to classical pantheons; and increasingly they are understood as genuine magical religious and social forces in the ancient world. But exactly how the gods and goddesses of the Celts interacted with each other and with their worshippers is a matter that has been given various and often contradictory interpretations. The Victorian scholars, to whom we owe a great deal, liked to generate inclusive rational systems, into which they then tried to fit or even force Celtic myths, legends and deities. Such systems do not always help us to approach and understand the inner nature of Celtic religion, mythology and magic.

SOLAR MYTHOLOGY AND SHAMANISM

One favourite Victorian system, still extensively applied today, was that of 'solar mythology', where every tale, character and symbolic attribute was assumed to be part of a solar and seasonal myth. In more recent times 'shamanism'[9] has become the catch-all term and, like solar mythology in the last century, it is often applied indiscriminately and without question to Celtic myth, religion and divine characters, heroes or magicians. There is no doubt whatsoever that powerful traditions of totem beasts, spirit flight and ancestor worship (which we shall encounter as we examine Celtic gods and goddesses) exist within Celtic tradition, even to the present day, deriving from pagan religion. Such traditions also form a major part of shamanism as recorded by anthropologists in the nineteenth and twentieth centuries: but this does not force us to the conclusion that Celtic religion was a type of shamanism, any more than the shamanistic elements in Tibetan Buddhism or even Roman Catholicism (such as totem animals of saints, mystical flights of vision and Jesuit techniques of visualization) would cause us to suggest that these major religions are 'shamanistic'. Both shamanism and the more pervasive theory of solar or seasonal mythology are present in Celtic religion, but only as organic elements closely interwoven with many other factors, rather than as major or inflexible rules.

Unfortunately for the convenient theory of solar mythology, even those Celtic gods that seem clearly to represent the sun are not solely part of a standard solar myth; this subtlety is found in classical pantheons also, for the life history of a god or goddess is an organic developing process, not a fully hatched, rigid list of emblems and attributes. So what can we say, by way of introduction, to help us approach the Celtic gods?

The Celtic Christ, stone cross from Duvillaun.

Many of the obvious questions, concerning roles, identities, relationships and significance, are not found by directly analysing lists of comparisons. There are many Celtic gods, for example, known from inscription or epigraphy and early literature, who equate with the classical Apollo or Mars, but hardly any of these are identical to the Greek forms that have become standardized ... indeed, the classical deities themselves showed variations which are often ignored in superficial interpretation. If we delve deeper into the history of Apollo, we find that he is likely to have been not a Greek god, but originally Celtic, so any rule-of-thumb comparisons are potentially invalid, as the interaction between Greek and Celtic peoples is complex and subtle. We shall return to the important figure of Apollo, and his major Celtic counterpart (or originator) the divine child Mabon, in later chapters.

POWERS AND PLACES

One of the methods of understanding Celtic deities is to remember that they are frequently local. There is an unfortunate tendency to assume that because a god or goddess is local he or she is therefore minor. This is a false conclusion, reflecting our conditioning to monotheism and political religion. Early Christian evangelists considered the *genii loci* or spirits of place to be minor forces or

demons: in later literature they became the cosy and vapid 'fairies' of Victorian sentiment ... which bear no relationship at all to the true fairy traditions from Celtic legend, some of which we shall discuss as we delve further into Celtic mythology. This evangelizing attitude was not merely a matter of propaganda or superior devotion to Christ: the Church fathers knew perfectly well that if a concept, image or god is belittled frequently, it begins to dwindle in the imagination of the worshippers. The early Church did not destroy pagan shrines, but booted out the residents and replaced them, admittedly with frequent failure and backsliding, with the unified new religion.

> Do not after all pull down the temples. Destroy the idols, purify the buildings with holy water, set relics there and let them become temples of the true God. So the people will have no need to change their places of concourse, and whereof they were wont to sacrifice cattle to demons, thither let them come on the day of the saint to whom the church is dedicated, and slay the beasts no longer as a sacrifice but for a social meal in honour of Him whom they now worship.
>
> Gregory the Great advising missionaries (from Bede's *History*).

The Celts had no problems whatsoever in the presence of many hundreds of entirely local gods and goddesses, and there is no validity in the assumption that such entities were necessarily minor because they were not found over large areas or regions or nations.

The goddess Sul or Sulis, for example, is known only at Aquae Sulis (Bath, England), yet her shrine was of such importance that the Romans built an amalgamated Romano–Celtic temple upon it, combining classical and local deities in profusion. Significantly a Roman *haruspex* or state augurer is known, from a dedication upon the surviving base of a lost statue, to have travelled to that far-flung outpost of the Empire to consult Sul and benefit from her oracular

21

powers. We know from his inscription that his request was answered. More important, Sulis was a local goddess, manifesting from the copious hot springs, who gave form to a widespread goddess well known to the Celts, Greeks and Romans alike. In other words, the local name or image was a specific and geomantic form for a higher or more universal archetype. This rule, in which localized and often unique deities are specific variants of greater god-forms, is important, but not by any means rigid or inevitable.

THE EVIDENCE

Much of our confusion over Celtic mythology is derived from lack of information ... the vast bulk of research and literature that has appeared in the last hundred years is, despite its apparent growth and complexity, derived from severely truncated and frequently suppressed and warped evidence. Nor should we blandly suggest that such suppression is a type of political Christian conspiracy ... the imperial pagan Romans also worked to amalgamate and reform Celtic religion before the dawning of the Christian era. But it is from the combined Roman and Celtic inscriptions and other early evidence assembled by archaeology that our fundamental factual evidence can be drawn. This is strongly localized, and we should never underestimate the *power of place* in Celtic myth and religion.

Head of the Celtic god of the Hot Springs at Aquae Sulis, Bath, England; similar to Belenos or Apollo. Often incorrectly labelled as 'Gorgon's head' or 'a male Medusa'.

The earliest factual sources, such as images, inscriptions, the remains of temples and the occasional writings of classical commentators upon Celtic culture, are supported by and compare significantly to British and Irish literature from approximately the seventh century to the late medieval period. Surprising as it may seem, a vast store of Celtic myth and legend was preserved by monastic chroniclers, and much of this compares in many details to the evidence of pre-Christian and early Christian sources.

To move further into this concept, we need to realize that to the Celts (and indeed to the ancient world generally) the land itself was a living sacred entity. There was no intellectual separation between 'religion' and 'living': all life, all acts, all relationships were essentially religious; not in any formal sense but as a matter of simple fact. Clearly there were formal religious sites; we know that the Druids set up sacred groves, and that the Romanized Celts built shrines and temples in the classical style, and that springs and wells were ancient potent worship sites. But these formalized locations were the nodes, so to speak, of energies within a living land, a land sacred as a goddess, and peopled by a host of visible and invisible supernatural entities. There is no suggestion here of crude 'animism' or 'superstition' ... such terms are far too simplistic and condescending.

During our exploration of the nature of Celtic gods and goddesses, and their relationship to the Celtic people whose lives were filled with such beings, we will not be assuming any type of primitivism or ignorance on the part of the Celts themselves. There is ample evidence that they were sophisticated and complex people, far indeed from the crude notion, still taught in some schools, that they were barbarians or savages until the Romans marched in to civilize them at the point of the sword.

MAJOR GODS AND GODDESSES

In addition to the important concept of 'locality', in which specific deities may occur only in relationship to a hill, spring, town, cave or other site, we need to consider the implications and evidence that there were indeed major god and goddess forms employed by the Celts. This does not necessarily mean that there was any formal unified religion that crossed tribal boundaries, for it seems likely from the evidence that local deities also represented local tribes, and that they fought with one another. We are dealing rather with a deep level of imagery, something which was shared in common by Celtic peoples without being formalized or unified.

Thus we find that mother goddesses, a fundamental of worship for humankind worldwide, had a major presence in all Celtic territories. The images and traditions of such goddesses, particularly as the essence or spirit of the land, were preserved well into historical times in Ireland, where the Great Goddess, known in many forms throughout the ancient pagan world, appears in Irish literature and poetry as the figure of Sovereignty.

The relationship between a king, his land, people and the Goddess, played an important role in Celtic culture. We find that as late as the twelfth century the Norman–Welsh writer Gerald du Barri (Gerald of Wales, also known as Giraldus Cambrensis) described a ritual in Donegal, Ireland, in which a tribal king was ceremonially 'married' to a mare[9]. This superficially bizarre tale falls into place

Ogham stone, carved with inscriptions in the ancient Celtic alphabet. From a churchyard at Kilmakedar, Dingle Peninsula, Co. Kerry, Ireland.

23

when we remember that one of the major Celtic goddesses was a horse goddess, often called Epona in European inscription. The horse was a major symbol of energy, power and fertility, and horse worship would perhaps have persisted from the earliest nomadic stages of proto-Celtic tribal culture.

Before moving on to specific examples of Celtic gods and goddesses, mythology and magic, we must briefly consider the cultural history of the Celtic peoples. Without this important background much of the mythology will be difficult to grasp; gods and goddesses are the direct result of interaction between people and places, formed in the imagination to act as vehicles for mysterious but real forces. Each race or nation has deeply rooted images shared among its members, formed and preserved over long periods of time, lying dormant even today, forgotten but not lost.

The Celts

The Celts are known to have occupied large territories in central Europe from at least as early as 800 BC, though proto-Celtic history reaches back a further millennium or more. Speculations as to Celtic origins are varied. During the nineteenth and early twentieth centuries scholars favoured a 'migratory' theory, in which Indo-European people gradually worked their way westwards over long periods of time; this viewpoint seems to have a certain validity in terms of cultural and religious affinities between the Celts and other Indo-European peoples, stretching as far east as the Indian subcontinent. This theory is still favoured by a number of modern writers, and has contributed towards valuable insights and studies of Celtic culture, religion and history[10].

But the migratory or diffusionist theory may be misleading through its superficial linear logic. It begs the question of actual origins and reduces it to one of movement. Modern scholars tend towards a more simple yet paradoxical viewpoint, that the Celts *emerged*, gradually developing their unique and recognizable Celtic characteristics, based upon foundations held in common by many other peoples, even as far afield as India. The similarities are not merely the result of ancient migrations, but due to properties of human consciousness – the way in which people relate to the land, to nature, and ultimately to the cosmos.

While racial groupings are clearly defined through long periods within certain areas, in which genetic patterns are firmly established, these groupings do not preclude a sharing of concepts and even important myths, which are found worldwide. This sharing is particularly evident in myths that involve stellar themes. Legends, rituals and festivals relating to the Pleiades, for example, are known in every part of the planet. This small group of stars was important in Celtic religion, and the rising and setting of the Pleiades in November and May marked the most significant annual festivals for the Celts, even as they do today for the primitive peoples of South America or Indonesia. The relationship between the Pleiades, seen as seven maidens, and Orion, who, in the role of a giant hunter, appears to chase the Pleiades across the sky, is the basis of a number of myths found in both Celtic and Greek religion. We find Celtic magical and prophetic traditions concerning Orion and the Pleiades as late as the bardic poems amalgamated into the twelfth-century *Prophecies of Merlin*[11].

This environmental and cosmological attitude is found throughout early

Celtic mythology, magic and culture, and gave rise to the religion, philosophy and the worship of gods and goddesses that people the Celtic world-view as expressions of forces and powers inherent in both humanity and the land itself, and the greater world of the stars.

In historical terms we know that early Celts occupied an area between the upper reaches of the rivers Elbe, Danube and Rhine, where traces of their culture may still be found. From this region they spread into northern Italy by around the sixth century BC. By 387 BC they had sacked Rome itself, in a memorable attack in which only the Capitol was unscathed. In the third century BC a far-reaching band of Celts penetrated into Greece, occupied the territory of Galatia, and eventually plundered the great oracular Underworld temple of Delphi. The plundering of Delphi is an event with many mythical undertones, for one of the primal Celtic myths, found in several forms, is that of a raid upon the Underworld. In such a raid, a band of heroes travels far into the mysterious potent realms that underpin nature, in pursuit of certain magical objects or powers. This theme was later attached to the Arthurian legends, and in early Welsh sources Arthur and a band of warriors seek possession of a magical cauldron in a raid upon Annwn, the Welsh Underworld. In later literature, this theme was to evolve and become refined as the Quest for the Holy Grail.

By the time Delphi had been raided, Celtic expansion had reached Gaul (south-western Europe), Spain, and Britain and Ireland. We should not imagine, however, that this extended territory, covering most of Europe from east to west, was a cohesive empire. The Celts moved in successive waves, under many different chieftains, often taking territories from one another as freely as from native non-Celtic peoples. The Celtic pattern of movement and conquest is long drawn out and decentralized ... the unity consisted of a religious, magical and cultural affinity, an affinity that in itself changed, developed and matured over centuries.

The Romans slowly conquered the Celtic territories in northern Italy, and eventually began to advance into Gaul, one of the most important developments

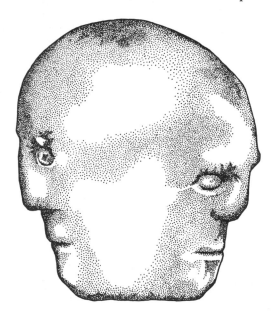

Two faces of a triple stone head from Corleck, Co. Cavan, Ireland.

26

Ritual mask from the sacred spring at Aquae Sulis, Bath, England. Similar masks are still used in folk rituals today in Britain and Europe, particularly in association with hobby horses and May ceremonies. Originally the mask would have been worn by a priest or priestess when speaking on behalf of a god or goddess.

in European history. In the second to first centuries BC, Gaul consisted of two regions which the Romans defined as Cis-Alpine and Trans-Alpine Gaul. The first region was that occupied by the Celts in northern Italy (south of the Alps, Gallia Cis-Alpina); the second consisted of France, Germany, Belgium and part of what is now Switzerland (Gallia Trans-Alpina). By the middle of the first century BC Julius Caesar, who provides us with some (perhaps second-hand) evidence concerning Celtic deities and culture, had conquered Gaul, which slowly became Romanized as a province[12]. The widespread independent Celtic territories in Europe were greatly reduced, and as the Romans made inroads into southern England and Wales 'pure' Celtic culture was confined to Ireland and northern Scotland. But, as we shall discover, the roots of Celtic culture run deep, and we should not imagine that either Gaul or southern Britain became rapidly or extensively Romanized, for there is ample evidence to the contrary.

It should be stated that just as there was no Celtic empire, there was no pure Celtic culture. What developed, in time, were certain 'pure' cultures in regions;

27

thus we might say that there was a strong and relatively unmixed Irish culture, as Ireland resisted non-Celtic conquest for several centuries. But the overall Celtic culture and peoples were a mixture of incoming and indigenous tribes, who eventually developed a linguistic and religious unity. It is this unity of language and myth, world-view and religious practice, that defines the early Celts just as much as their unique artistic skills, which underwent several periods of transformation, the last being as late as the Christian era.

When Caesar began the conquest and absorption of Gaul into the Roman Empire, the Celtic culture was held together by language and religion, particularly by the Druidic system, to which we shall return later. Caesar himself stated that the Druids originated in Britain, and when Druidic practices were outlawed by Rome, troublesome Druids frequently appeared to foment rebellion by making the short sea crossing between Britannia and Gaul[13]. Although Caesar invaded England, a true conquest was not achieved until the invasion by Claudius in AD 43–7; thereafter a British province was created that extended as far north as the region between the rivers Forth and Clyde in southern Scotland.

To this day the Antonine Wall, erected by the Roman government as a barrier against the savage northern tribes, may still be seen. By the reign of Commodus, AD 180–92, Hadrian's Wall (begun around AD 130) had become the northern boundary line. Thus the primal un-Romanized Celtic culture or tribes persisted well into the Roman period. There is a famous account by Tacitus of a Roman expedition against the Druid sanctuary or college of Anglesey in AD 61; the historian, perhaps with a touch of dramatic improvisation, describes black-robed Druidesses[14] cursing the faltering Roman legionaries:

> Suetonius Paulinus therefore prepared to attack the island of Mona [Anglesey], which had a powerful population and was a refuge for [Celtic] fugitives. He built flat-bottomed vessels to cope with the shallows and uncertain depths of the sea. Thus the infantry crossed while the cavalry followed by fording, or, where the water was deep, swam by the side of their horses.
>
> On the shore stood the opposing army with its dense array of armed warriors, while between the ranks dashed women, in black attire like the Furies, with hair dishevelled, waving brands. All around, the Druids, lifting up their hands to heaven, and pouring forth imprecations, scared our soldiers by the unfamiliar sight, so that, as if their limbs were paralysed, they stood motionless, and exposed to wounds. Then urged by their general's appeals and mutual encouragements not to quail before a troop of frenzied women, they bore the standards onwards, smote down all resistance, and wrapped the foe in the flames of his own brands. A force was next set over the conquered, and their groves, devoted to inhuman superstitions, were destroyed. They deemed it indeed a duty to cover their altars with the blood of captives and to consult their deities through human entrails.　　　　(Tacitus, *The Annals*, trans. Church and Brodribb, 1895)

If, as seems to be the case, many of these soldiers were in fact Celtic mercenaries from Gaul, they would certainly have been wary of attacking a Druidic college. Anglesey is a large island off the coast of north Wales, and while this was being attacked, a mixed Romano–Celtic culture was well under way in southern Britain, though not without regular opposition from the fiercely independent Celts. Indeed, the famous rebellion of the red-haired warrior queen Boudicca[15] exploded against injustice in southern England at about the same time as Suetonius Paulinus led his soldiers across the Menai Straits to Anglesey. As with

The Gündestrup Cauldron, perhaps the most impressive and famous Celtic artifact known. Cauldrons are found in many Celtic legends as magical vessels of regeneration. The Gündestrup Cauldron is a ritual object, made of silver, which displays its own detailed myth and ceremony. On one internal panel, a parade of warriors is being plunged into a cauldron, probably for regeneration after death.

so many Celtic actions, Boudicca wove certain religious or magical elements into her uprising, including the use of a hare as totem animal, and the execution of opponents as sacrifices to the fierce goddess Andraste.

EARLIEST RECORDS OF THE CELTS

Celtic culture in its prototypical examples is known as early as the Bronze Age, by which time it seems to have reached as far west as Britain and Ireland. Archaeologists and linguists define two Celtic language groups, which have many affinities, but certain recognizable differences. The Gaelic or Gadhelic speech employs what is popularly known as 'Q-Celtic', the origin of modern Gaelic. The Gauls and Brythons to the south spoke what is known as 'P-Celtic', replacing the 'q', 'k', or 'c' sound in many examples with a 'p' sound. Thus the Gadhelic word *mac* or *maqvi*, meaning 'son of', becomes *map* in Welsh, or *mab*. The 'm' may be dropped to give the term *ap* found in many medieval Welsh names.

Q-Celtic is found today in Irish and Scots Gaelic, and in Manx. P-Celtic survives in Welsh, Breton (closely related to ancient Welsh), and the practically extinct Cornish language. When we examine the names of Celtic gods and goddesses, we shall find examples of P-Celtic and Q-Celtic, and the linguistic differences do not necessarily imply major cultural differences.

The Gadhelic Celts or Goidels seem to have been the first tribes to reach the furthest west in Europe. They arrived in Ireland, possibly from Spain (as Irish tradition suggests), in the prehistoric period; this factual migration is echoed in the legendary *Book of Invasions*, which fuses myth and history with cosmology, in a poetic and originally Druidic explanation of the history of the land as a sacred entity into which various types of being appear until the human races eventually dominate (see pages 126–37).

The final wave of Gadhelic movement was as late as the fifth century AD, when they travelled from Ireland to Dalriada (now Argyllshire in Scotland). This late movement was the origin of the Scottish race, for the migrants were *scotti*, a term meaning fighters or skirmishers. They merged with the aboriginal proto-Celtic Picts, and eventually became the dominant culture, absorbing the old Pictish peoples completely. Many of the chthonic (earth-related) elements of Celtic mythology, however, such as the Underworld and ancestor worship, would have been carried over from such earlier peoples, being religious themes held in common by races throughout the Western world.

The P-Celts, or Brythonic tribes, made their major western movements during the Iron Age. The most famous example of their culture is found at Hallstadt in Austria, on an extensive site first excavated in 1846, and still being examined today. The Hallstadt culture is one of our most significant sources for information on the Celts, and reveals the transition from a bronze- to an iron-based culture. In the Iron Age proper, around 500 BC, we have the evidence of the La Tène culture, from Switzerland, and from the Marne valley in France. This great period of Celtic civilization reveals skill in metal and artwork of the highest kind. Many of the designs typical to the La Tène culture spread widely over Europe[16].

The last Celtic invasions and movements before the Romanization of Gaul were those of the Belgae, between approximately 100 and 50 BC. These were a vigorous warlike Celtic people. They developed lowland agriculture, clearing forests, using wheeled ploughs, acting as overlords to existing Celtic tribes in the regions which they conquered. It was the Belgic rulers, in a political sense, that were conquered by the Romans.

Celtic rulers were often elected, and the high chief or overlord chosen by the tribes to oppose Caesar was a Belgic leader, Cassivellaunus. This simple historical fact leads into the complex theme of Celtic kingship, to which we shall return during our chapters on religion and magic, gods and goddesses. The king was essentially responsible for the well-being of the land and people within the land, by his relationship to the goddess of the land or territory. This was not a nebulous formality, but a very real belief with many practical implications for Celtic government and politics. Celtic kings were elected as late as the eleventh century, for Macbeth was an elected king after the ancient Celtic manner, proving to be a competent and effective ruler, very different from the insane tyrant described in Shakespeare's play of the same name[17].

Thus, by the Roman period in Gaul and southern Britain, we find a complex but generally unified culture, in which successive waves of Celtic tribes, over long periods of time, have amalgamated with one another. These peoples had a complex and often highly developed culture, and were not primitive in the sense of being crude or unsophisticated.

They had developed all the cultural skills of metal-working, agriculture, farming, pottery, art, trade, and in some cases major building, though Celtic culture tended not to centralize upon cities. The Celts were great seafarers, and as Caesar himself attests in a famous passage in his *Gallic Wars*, the Veneti (in Brittany) were far superior in their shipbuilding and sailing skills to the Romans.

> The ships of the Gauls were built and rigged in a style different from our own. They were constructed with flatter bottoms to enable them to pass through shallow water in

Apollo, from the Temple of Sulis Minerva, Bath. Built into the medieval church at Compton Dando, some miles from its original location. Apollo was equated with the Celtic god Mabon or Maponus, the Son of Light, who was widely worshipped in Britain and Gaul.

shoals or ebb tides. Their very high bows and sterns made them fit for use in heavy seas and violent gales, and with hulls made throughout of oak they were able to stand innumerable shocks and rough use. Their cross-timbers, made of beams a foot wide, were made fast with iron bolts the width of a man's thumb. Their anchors were held not with ropes but with iron chains. Their sails were made of raw hides or thin leather, either because they were ignorant or lacked flax, or, as seems more likely, because they knew that ordinary sails would not withstand the violent storms and winds of the Atlantic, and were not suited to such heavy vessels in any case. In meeting the Veneti the only advantage our Roman ships had was that they were faster and could be driven by strength of oars; in every other respect the ships of the enemy were far better adapted for sailing in their treacherous and stormy waters. We could not damage them by ramming as they were so solid; their height made it difficult for us to fire missiles into them or to grapple and board them. Furthermore, when it began to blow and they ran before the wind, they weathered the blast more easily. They could come-to in shallow waters with greater safety, and when grounded by the receding tide had no fear of pointed rocks of reefs . . . while to our ships all these risks were daunting.

(From Julius Caesar, *Gallic Wars*)

The war chariot was used extensively by certain Celtic tribes, delivering warriors rapidly to the front, where they dismounted and fought on foot. In addition to classical descriptions of the chariot, it features strongly in heroic Celtic tradition, drawn from oral or collective poetic sources.

When Cuchulainn's shape changing frenzy was over, he leaped into his scythed chariot equipped with iron points, with thin edges, with hooks, with hard spit-spikes, with machinery for opening it, with sharp nails that studded over its axles and straps and curved parts and tackles. Then he delivered a thunder feat of one hundred, and one of two hundred, one of three hundred, one of four hundred, and stood at the thunder feat of five hundred. And he went so far because he felt it to be obligatory upon him that in this, his first set-to and grappling with the army of the four provinces of Erin, even such a number must fall by his hand. So he went forward to assault his enemies, giving the chariot such force that its iron shod wheel sank in the earth and made ruts which might well have served as earthworks of defence; for both stones and rocks, both flagstones and the earth's bottom-gravel on either hand were heaped up outside the wheels to an equal height with them.

(The Chariot of Cuchulainn from 'The Cattle Raid of Cooley', *The Cuchulainn Saga*, edited by Eleanor Hull)

While the Celts were not organized in a centralized and politically unified manner as the Romans were, they certainly had extensive skills and civilization. It was, perhaps, the independence and de-centralization of the Celtic culture that led to its downfall, as it could not, by its nature, withstand the increasingly depersonalized imperial might of Rome. The Celts, wildly flamboyant, eccentric, proud, ritualistic and magically inspired, were simply unable to present a coherent continuous opposition to the Roman invaders. It was, essentially, only a matter of time before the Roman military machine wore the Celts down, no matter how many heroic deeds and uprisings were undertaken. We know from Caesar that if the Celts had been met solely on the open field of battle, their traditional ritualized place of war, their eventual defeat would have been less certain. But the Romans practised a 'no-holds-barred' type of warfare, far removed from the ritualized single combat and heroic rules of the Celts; Caesar went to remarkable lengths to reduce the Celts in Europe, using methods that simply would never occur to Celtic warrior chieftains or kings, and which would be, perhaps, considered sacrilegious if we remember the Celtic root concept of the sanctity of the land.

> Caesar constructed elaborate siege works [to contain the Celtic king Vercingetorix]. He had a trench dug twenty feet in width, with perpendicular sides, as wide at the top as at the bottom. The other earthworks were kept some six hundred and fifty yards behind this trench, to protect them against surprise attacks, for such a vast extent of ground had to be enclosed that it was difficult to man the entire circuit, and there was a danger of the enemy charging down in force upon the lines at night, or hurling javelins during the day when the men were occupied with entrenching. At this distance, then, Caesar had two trenches dug of equal depth, each being fifteen feet wide, and filled the innermost, where it crossed the low ground of the plain, with water diverted from the streams. Behind the trenches a rampart with palisades was constructed, reinforced by a battlemented breastwork, with large forked branches protruding where it joined the rampart to obstruct the enemy if they tried to climb over it. Towers were then built at intervals of one hundred and thirty yards along the entire circuit of fortification. . . . When these defences were finished, Caesar constructed a similar line of fortifications facing outwards instead of inwards. This line made a circuit of fourteen miles, running along the most level ground that could be used, and it was designed to hold off attacks from outside, so that even if the cavalry of Vercingetorix came in strength, the Roman troops defending the siege works would not be surrounded.
> (From Julius Caesar, *Gallic Wars*)

MYTHS OF THE CELTS

Almost all of our information on Celtic mythology comes from second- or third-hand sources, or is obtained by deduction from speculating upon even further removed examples of folklore, superstition and the like. Originally Celtic religion was preserved *orally*; this is a most important concept for the reader to bear in mind, for we are so totally accustomed to having information stored in writing, or nowadays in computer bytes, that it is difficult to comprehend a culture in which the written word was either unknown or regarded as a trivializing influence. Nevertheless, this is the situation that we must consider when we think of the earliest stages of Celtic culture. We know from classical sources that Druids did not write matters down, but preserved immense stores of learning through memory alone. A well-defined art of memory was known in the classical world, where it seems to have been closely allied to a visual imaginative system of storing information; the progress of this art from classical times to the Renaissance is examined in detail by Frances A. Yates in her book *The Art of Memory* (published by Routledge and Kegan Paul).

By the time Caesar was writing about the Druids, however, the fact that their laws and traditions were oral and that writing was seldom used was already remarkable to the Romans, and the orator's art of memory seems to have become something of technical curiosity rather than a feature of daily life.

We do know, as a result of fairly modern research, that the Celts had a simple alphabetic system called 'Ogham'. Much nonsense has been written in recent years concerning both Ogham and the much later writing system of the Norse runes. Both were, no matter what extravagant claims have been made, very basic symbol systems for preserving alphabets. Undoubtedly alphabets were regarded as magical, and many correspondences attached to them, yet the Celtic magical or mystical alphabet consisted not of letters or symbols, but of orders of living beings, plants, animals, humans and non-humans. The traditions of such organic alphabets are preserved in a number of Celtic early poems and legends from both Britain and Ireland.

Certain ancient inscriptions are found in Ogham upon stones, in Ireland and Britain, and if the theories of Professor Barry Fell (*America BC*, Pocket Books, New York) are correct, there are inscriptions in Celtic Ogham on ancient stones upon the eastern seaboard of America.

An important tract on Ogham, *The Scholar's Primer*[18], which consists of several texts dating back to traditions from the sixth century or earlier, reveals that there were many ways of using this alphabetic system . . . two initiates into its simple mysteries could converse openly with one another by finger patterns, or even by rubbing fingers across the bridges of their noses! In this sense Ogham is similar in concept (though not in pattern) to the modern sign language used by deaf or mute people.

But we need not imagine a Celtic society in which lengthy inscriptions were found cut upon every tree or stone: Ogham seems to have been reserved for important funerary inscriptions or for god names, and occasional permanent statements. We may consider a system in which a few key images or names or codes were inscribed in Ogham, and these in turn led to key lines (such as the Welsh *Triads*[19]), which helped to open out the vast repertoire of traditional lore kept only in the bardic or druidic memory.

Whatever the situation regarding alphabets, there is no doubt that the mythology of the early Celts was not preserved in writing, at least not until the tantalizing hints that we find from Romanized inscriptions. Even these are limited to local names conflated with classical names . . . and the combination is sometimes confusing, and not necessarily logical. It seems clear, from inscriptions such as the famous altar to Esus and the Tarvos Trigarnus, that the Roman words were mere multi-cultural tags to a mythic system which was well known. Such inscriptions were mainly confined to the grander state temples, though they are also known from domestic and smaller locations.

Some of the best sources of insight into Celtic mythology are monastic records

Taranis, the Wheel God, as shown on the pagan Gündestrup Cauldron. The winged creatures in the foreground persisted in Celtic art until as late as the Christian era. Compare with example from the monastery on Iona on page 119.

kept by early Irish Christians: the great tales, poems, sagas, or cycles of legend, preserved by pagan Celtic poets, were written down by their Christian associates . . . or perhaps the poets themselves, when they became monks, wrote out their lore to preserve it.

The Irish poets, known as *filid*, were a guild deriving loosely from the old Druidic orders; they made independent laws and maintained an internal discipline exempt from those laws applying to commoners. As late as AD 590 there was a popular outcry against the *filid* in Ireland, but they were supported by no less a person than St Columba, also trained as a *fili*, and allowed to continue to practise with certain restrictions upon their rights. Within this highly autocratic society of poets, the use of Ogham preserved elements of secrecy and mnemonic skills. The Irish *filid* were more or less the equivalent of the British bards, and throughout this book we use the term 'bard' as a generic word for those professional poets, either within or without formal schools, who preserved lore from the pagan Celtic or Druidic traditions well into the Christian historical period.

Whatever the reasons, a vast heritage of Irish mythology was preserved in ecclesiastical texts. Despite the re-writing of certain themes and characters that were too overtly pagan, there is substantial and clear evidence of pagan mythology in these Irish sources, which never came under Roman rule. Surprisingly, they compare very well to the more limited classical and Romano–Celtic evidence that we have from a much earlier period. We may conclude, therefore, that the traditions of Celtic myth and legend (drawn from pagan Celtic religion) retained many central elements for a very long period – at least from the first century BC to the tenth century AD. The classical and imperial evidence is founded, of course, upon traditions already in existence, so we may reasonably suggest a mythic continuity to Celtic religion from at least 1,000 BC to AD 1,000. Many writers would propose a longer period, extending parallels back into the Bronze Age to *c.* 3,000 BC.

In Britain, the Romans established rulership throughout most of the south, parts of Wales, and an uneasy dominance in the far north of England, without

Cernunnos, the Lord of the Animals, on the Gündestrup Cauldron. The small figure riding a dolphin is reminiscent of a number of sea gods in European mythology, and may represent a god similar to the Welsh Dylan, child of the waves.

reaching deeply into Scotland. The Romano–British inscriptions, dedications and images of Celtic or amalgamated gods and goddesses frequently follow the Gaulish pattern, but with typical regional and local unique examples that we expect to find in the de-centralized environmentally attuned Celtic religion. Wales preserved many of the British Celtic myths in a cycle of tales and poems that persisted as bardic entertainments into the Middle Ages. The most famous collection, now called the *Mabinogion*, contained considerable evidence of Celtic myth, magic and pagan lore. Similar material abounds in the books of Geoffrey of Monmouth, who wrote an extensive legendary *History of the British Kings*[20] in the twelfth century, and two very important but virtually unknown books concerning Merlin, the *Prophecies* and the *Life* of Merlin. (These texts have been examined in detail in *The Prophetic Vision of Merlin* and *The Mystic Life of Merlin*, R. J. Stewart, Arkana, 1986). The Merlin texts preserve in an expanded and often confused form a mass of bardic or Druidic lore, cosmology, magical images, incantations, prophecies, and many mythic episodes, loosely woven around the central figure of Merlin, who was renowned as a seer and prophet among the Welsh and southern Scots from at least as early as the fifth century onwards. We shall return to Merlin in a separate chapter (see page 102).

The Celts and Nature

In the sixth century, the Christian chronicler Gildas wrote that the British people blindly worshipped mountains, rivers and springs. Relationship with nature, with the land and its non-human inhabitants, is central to Celtic religion. The condemnation of nature worship originates with Christian dogma and the spread of monotheism; in later centuries nature worship was again denigrated as superstition, but from a materialist or rationalist viewpoint.

Yet no modern scientist, ecologist or biologist would deny that we have ignored and abused nature, the land, the environment, at our greatest peril. The ancients saw nature as a living entity, and the spirits, gods and goddesses were forms or manifestations of the living land, the living planet in the solar system and ultimately in the stellar universe.

The primal understanding of a living land, in which humans and many other beings from plants to animals to invisible entities, all related to one another, was held in common by all ancient cultures. Certain features and developments, however, may be recognized as Celtic, and a host of gods and goddesses are known from Celtic traditions and inscriptions.

ROOTS WITHIN THE UNDERWORLD

Most primal cults and beliefs have a very direct foundation; the Earth and the Underworld[21]. The primal deity was an earth goddess, the Mother; we find this theme in both classical and Celtic religion. The Celts gave the Earth Mother many localized names, often associated with specific sites. While such names seem confusing to us, a pagan Celt travelling from region to region in Europe, Britain or Ireland, would understand that the local forms were variants of the fundamental concept of a mother goddess, and would honour her according to both local and general custom. Goddesses, like many other Celtic concepts or images, tended to become triplicated. In Romanized Gaul and Britain we find inscriptions to the *Matres*, who were also defined in Britain. Ireland, which never experienced Roman conquest, likewise defined goddesses in triple form, confirming that this was a widespread tendency among the Celts and not inherited from the classical world, which also had ancient traditions of goddesses in triple form.

The major significance of the Underworld is probably derived from a very early period indeed, and was held in common between the Celtic and pre-Celtic inhabitants of Europe. In brief, it was understood that all energy, life, power, and death came from beneath the ground. A goddess ruled this potent realm, but she would also have had a consort, sons and daughters. Many myths and legends, found as late as the medieval period, reflected this primal tradition. Worship sites were frequently located upon springs, wells and caves, which were the entrances to the Underworld or Otherworld.

SPIRITS OF THE LAND

Natural features of any region attracted and generated myths, for the forces of nature were given imaginative forms by the Celts. Many of the names of Celtic deities merely reflect their location, but this is also a key to their power, for the name, place and power were three strands woven inseparably together.

TREES AND DRUIDS

Forests held an especial significance for the ancient peoples, and tree worship seems to be a major feature within Celtic religion . . . though, like the Underworld tradition, it stems from a primal origin that predates the Celts themselves. It is difficult for modern people to grasp fully the power of the vast forests that covered Europe; a primeval forest has a distinct and powerful feeling of entity and vitality, and such forests were a major feature of the life of the Celts.

In popular misconceptions, the Druids are associated with stone circles, but the megalithic religious monuments long predate the apperace of Celts or Druids. The Druids were an aristocratic priesthood, generally divided into three orders, corresponding loosely to our modern terms Judges, Prophets and Poets. A Druidic decision or judgement was the ultimate form of Celtic law, defined by tradition, orally preserved precedents, and poetic inspiration.

The classical description, given by Pliny, associates Druids, and therefore Celts, with tree worship:

> Nothing is more sacred to the druids than the mistletoe and the tree on which it grows, especially if it be an oak. They seek the oak tree for their sacred groves, and no

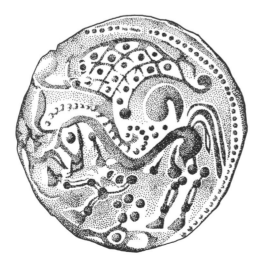

Stylized horse on Celtic coin from the Jura region.

38

ceremony is complete without its branches. Whatever grows on the tree is sent from heaven, a sign that the tree has been chosen by the god.

Traditions concerning the oak, mistletoe and the fruitful powers of earth and heaven are found throughout the ancient world. Maximus of Tyre stated that a giant oak was revered 'as Zeus' by the Celts, by which he meant not the Greek god Zeus, but the Celtic equivalent who performed similar functions — a god associated with thunder, lightning and oak trees, a Sky Father to consort with the Earth Mother. This is, in fact, the god defined in the Romano—Celtic period as Taranis the thunderer, god of the Wheel of the Seasons or Stars.

Groves were especially sacred, and this reverence for groves and trees persisted in Ireland until a very late date, and is preserved in folklore even today. Sacred trees, called *bile*, either of oak or ash, were sacrosanct in Ireland, and to cut one down was a terrible crime. We find this motif reflected in magical ballads such as 'The Two Brothers', still preserved in oral tradition in the twentieth century, in which one brother kills another as retribution for 'cutting down a little hazel bush that might have grown into a tree'.

How come that blood on the point of your sword
My son come and tell to me?
Oh it is the blood of a little song bird
That sat in yonder tree tree tree
That sat in yonder tree.

But a little bird's blood it was never so red
My son come and tell to me?
Oh it is the blood of my own greyhound
That would not run for me me me
That would not run for me.

But a greyhound's blood it was never so rare
My son come and tell to me?
Oh it is the blood of my gray mare
That would not ride for me me me
That would not ride for me.

But a gray mare's blood it was never so clear
My son come and tell to me?
Oh it is the blood of my own brother dear
That rode away with me me me,
That rode away with me.

And what did you two fall out about,
My son come and tell to me?
Oh it was that he plucked up a little hazel bush
That should have grown to a tree tree tree
That should have grown to a tree.

And what will you do when your father comes to know
My son come and tell to me?
Oh I'll set foot in a bottomless boat
And sail and sail across the sea
And sail across the sea.

And when will you be coming back again,
My son come and tell to me?
When Moon and Sun dance in yonder hill
And that will never be be be
And that will never be.

(Traditional ballad widespread in
Britain and North America)

Such ballads contain many relics from Celtic tradition, and the 'two brothers' theme occurs again in the Grail legends, those of Merlin, and other medieval tales that retain and partly retell Celtic myth from pagan origins. The motif of cutting down a tree is ancient; a Romano–Celtic altar to the god Esus shows a man cutting down a tree, and the motif is further associated with three birds and a bull. When we find similar imagery occurring in legend and later folklore, we are following the tenuous but persistent thread of a half-forgotten myth connected to a Celtic god.

Sacred trees often grew over sacred springs or wells: this was a literal and physical manifestation of a magical and universal concept. Thus the physical tree and well were sacred sources of power, for they connected the Underworld, the Land, and the Overworld of sky and stars together. They also represented a cosmic vision of unity, the World Tree reaching into the stars. This important concept, also shown as the *axis mundi* in medieval and Renaissance texts, is typified by three worlds or levels, reaching through moon, sun and stars. In British Druidic tradition there seems to have been a similar concept of three worlds, preserved in Welsh tradition; each world contained its own orders of inhabitants.

Trees are still decorated with offerings today in parts of Ireland, Scotland and Brittany, ostensibly dedicated to Christian saints who have taken over the guardianship of certain revered healing wells and springs. The trees around such holy water sources are hung with strips of coloured cloth, prayers or similar modest tokens in a tradition of offering and supplication that may be traced back to the pre-Christian Celtic era.

WATER AND SACRED HEADS

River, wells, springs and lakes, were all sacred power sources to the Celts. In such water sources dwelt not only energy, but divine and semi-divine beings, giving form and expression to the geomantic and otherworld energies that were interwoven upon any specific location. Sources were also regarded as the entrances to the Underworld, through which even humans might pass into the mysterious lands and realms of power. The Romans robbed the lakes of Gaul of their great treasures, and even auctioned the lakes prior to conquest, so well known was the Celtic habit of laying up offerings and wealth in water sources. The geographer Strabo (54 BC–AD 21) quotes from the Greek writer Posidonius as follows:

> . . . as Posidonius and many others have said, the country [of Gaul] being rich in gold, with inhabitants fearing the gods and living frugally, possessed treasures in many parts of the Celtic realm, and the lakes in particular provided inviolability for their treasures, into which they let down heavy masses of gold and silver. The Romans, indeed, when they conquered the region, sold off the lakes by public auction.

(Strabo, IV 13)

Primal god figure with radiant hair or halo, from Northern Ireland.

In Wales, the copious archaeological finds from Llyn Cerrig Bach, Anglesey, including objects as large as chariots, may be derived from a sacred source originally connected to Druid worship. The college on Anglesey was suppressed by Suetonius Paulinus in AD 61, and archaeologists have suggested that the vast hoard may have been part of a desperate magical attempt to fend off the invaders ... though it seems just as likely that it accumulated as described by Strabo in the quote given above.

Water worship was often very specific, frequently connected to therapy. Many models of parts of the body have been found at Celtic worship sites; these were deposited in the sacred springs as offerings or pleas to the powers. Inscriptions were also found, after the influence of Roman culture. At Aquae Sulis (Bath) in Britain, the goddess Sulis Minerva presided over both therapy and cursing, as is well attested by inscribed lead plaques in her honour. She was also associated with prophecy, for she was a goddess of the Underworld, where all powers flow together and the future and past are as one. The name Sul or Sulis is Q-Celtic for a gap, orifice or eye.

The therapeutic power of wells remained into historical Christian times, with saints taking over but never quite disguising pagan functions. Rituals were preserved in folklore deriving from pagan worship; these include processing around wells, making offerings, models of limbs (as in ancient Celtic practice known from archaeological evidence), and ceremonies involving drinking from skulls. This last custom links directly to the pagan Celtic belief in the sanctity of the head.

The earliest Celts were head hunters, preserving the trophies in cedar oil; a feature of the Irish sagas such as the legends of Cuchulainn is the potency of the head both as a source of power and as a totem or trophy. Cuchulainn, the Hound of Ulster, undergoes a magical transformation in which a fountain of terrible power erupts from his head, while other Celtic heroes converse or utter prophecies after their death and decapitation[22]. The theme is developed in the *Mabinogion* with the head of Bran which converses with his companions, and is set as a magical guardian of the Land of Britain upon the White Hill in London.

In consequence of that [battle with the Men of Ireland] the men of the Island of the Mighty [Britain] were not victorious, for only seven men of them all escaped and Bendigeid Vran himself was wounded in the foot with a poisoned dart. The seven men that escaped were Pryderi, Manawyddan, Gluneu Eil Taran, Taliesin, Ynawc, Grudyen the son of Muryel, and Heilyn the son of Gwynn Hen.

And Bendigeid Vran commanded them to cut off his head. 'And do you take my head,' he said, 'and bear it even unto the White Mount, in London, and bury it there with the face towards France. And a long time will you be upon the road. In Harlech you will be feasting seven years, the birds of Rhiannon singing unto you the while. And all that time the head will be to you as pleasant company as ever it was when it was on my body. And at Gwales in Penvro you will be fourscore years, and you may remain there, and the head will remain with you uncorrupted, until you open the door that looks towards Aber Henvelen, and towards Cornwall. And after you have opened that door, there you may no longer tarry, set forth then to London to bury the head, and go straight forward.' So they cut off his head, and those seven went forward therewith ...

Then they went on to Harlech, and there stopped to rest, and they provided meat and liquor, and sat down to eat and drink. And there came three birds, and they began singing a certain song, and all the songs those men had ever heard were unpleasant compared thereto; and the birds seemed to them to be at a great distance from them over the sea, yet they appeared as distinct as if they were close by, and at this feast they continued for seven years.

And at the close of the seventh year they went forth to Gwales in Penvro. And there they found a fair and regal spot overlooking the ocean, and a spacious hall therein. And they went into the hall, and two of its doors were open, but the third door was closed, that which looked towards Cornwall. 'See yonder,' said Manawyddan, 'is the door that we may not open.' And that night they regaled themselves and were joyful. And of all they had seen of food laid before them, and of all they had heard of, they remembered nothing, neither of that, nor of any sorrow whatsoever. And they remained in that place fourscore years, unconscious of having ever spent a time more joyous and mirthful. And they were not more weary than when first they came, neither did any of them know the time that they had been there. And it was not more irksome to them having the head with them, than if Bendigeid Vran himself had been with them. And because of the fourscore years, it was called The Entertaining of the Noble Head . . .

One day Heilyn the son of Gwynn said, 'Evil betide me if I do not open that door to discover if that is true which is said concerning it!' So he opened the door and looked towards Cornwall and Aber Henvelen. And when they had looked, they became as conscious of all the evils they had ever sustained, and of all the friends and companions

Primitive relief carving of the Triple Goddess, from the area of Aquae Sulis. The three figures represent the basic pattern of Maiden, Mother and Crone.

they had lost, and of all the misery that had befallen them, as if all had happened in that very spot; and especially were they conscious of the fate of their lord. And because of their misery they could not rest, but journeyed forth with the head of Vran towards London. And they buried the head in the White Mount, and when it was buried, this was the Third Goodly Concealment; and it was the Third Ill-Fated Disclosure when it was disinterred, inasmuch as no invasion came from across the sea to this island [of Britain] while the head was in that concealment.

(From 'Branwen the Daughter of Llyr', *The Mabinogion*, translated by Lady Charlotte Guest)

A number of shrines containing or intended for sacred heads are known from pagan Celtic culture, as is shown by archaeological evidence. The use of a blessed or holy skull was preserved in several holy wells in Britain and Ireland until as late as the eighteenth or nineteenth century. The sacred skull, which also features in the medieval Christian practice of holy relics, further links the sacred well with the cult of the dead or ancestors, a major feature of Celtic belief that we shall examine in later chapters. The theme of the blessed ancestors runs through all Celtic mythology and magic, though the boundaries between gods, goddesses, ancestors, and fairies are often blurred.

The largest body of water is, of course, the sea. In addition to river goddesses and gods, the Celts had certain well-defined sea deities. These included Llyr, Manannan and Dylan, who are discussed in later chapters. Celtic sea gods appeared in medieval literature, particularly in the Arthurian romances, which

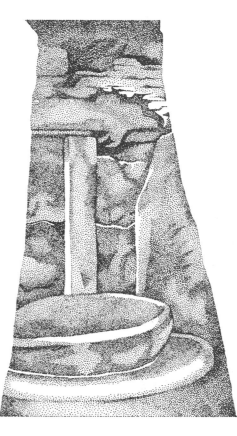

The North side of the Bronze Age ritual chamber of Newgrange, Ireland. Traditionally known as the Bruigh na Boinne, this chamber was said to be the Underworld dwelling or *sidh* of the god Oenghus, the Irish Son of Light. The bowl is made of stone.

43

disguised vast stores of Celtic tradition deriving from the story-cycles once circulated by professional bards. In Geoffrey of Monmouth's *Vita Merlini* (1150), for example, we find a thinly disguised Celtic sea god, called Barinthus[23], who ferries the wounded King Arthur to the Fortunate Island. Such sea gods have a curious and often loosely defined role as stellar deities. This may derive from the importance of stars in navigation to sea-faring people, but also has a deeper significance connected to the observation of stellar phenomena which occupied so much of our ancestors' religious and magical beliefs and practices.

MOON, SUN AND STARS

Although it has been fashionable to rationalize the stories of certain Celtic gods as 'solar worship', the evidence of actual sun or moon worship is not great in a

Partial reconstruction of Celtic temple portico, from Roquepertuse (Bouches-du-Rhône), third or fourth century BC. The early Celts were head hunters, and the head was regarded as a sacred and potent object.

44

Celtic context. The famous Coligny calendar, a Celtic calculating calendar found in France (at Coligny near Lyons) seems to have been used to synchronize the lunar and solar years, and is not in itself evidence of worship but of a developed culture using calendars and calculations. The Coligny calendar also features positive and negative phases and periods, showing clearly the Celtic concern with polarity, and this concern is found on many levels deeper than that of mere superstition. We find the concept of polarity reflected in many legends, and two typical scenes from the *Mabinogion* demonstrate this well:

And when they came to the middle of the ford of the Severn, Iddawc turned his horse's head, and Rhonabwy looked along the valley of the Severn. And he beheld two fair troops coming towards the ford. One troop of brilliant white, whereof every one of the men had a scarf of white satin with jet black borders. And the knees and the tops of the shoulders of their horses were jet black, though they were of pure white in every other part. And their banners were pure white, with black points to them all . . .

And further on he saw a troop, whereof each man wore garments of jet black, with borders of pure white to every scarf, and the tops of the shoulders and the knees of their horses were pure white. And their banners were jet black with pure white at the point of each . . .

And after he had dismounted he heard a great tumult and confusion amongst the host, and such as were then at the flanks turned in towards the centre, and such as had been in the centre strove to reach the flanks. And then, behold, he saw a knight coming, clad, both he and his horse, in mail, of which the rings were whiter than the whitest lily, and the rivets redder than the ruddiest blood. And this man rode at the heart of the host.

'Iddawc,' said Rhonabwy, 'Is the host fleeing?' 'The man whom thou seest yonder is Kai. He is the fairest horseman in all of King Arthur's court, and the men who are at the front of the army hasten to the rear to see Kai ride, and the men who are at the centre of the army flee forwards to avoid the shock of his mighty horse. And this is the cause of the movement and confusion of the host.'

(From 'The Dream of Rhonabwy', *The Mabinogion*,
translated by Lady Charlotte Guest)

Peredur rode on towards a river valley whose edges were forested, with level meadows on both sides of the river. On one bank there was a flock of white sheep, and on the other a flock of black sheep. When a white sheep bleated a black sheep would cross the river and turn white, and when a black sheep bleated a white sheep would cross the river and turn black. On the bank of the river he saw a tall tree: from roots to crown one half was aflame and the other green with leaves.

(From 'Peredur Son of Evrawg', *The Mabinogion*,
translated by Jeffrey Gantz)

The primal Celtic cycle seems to be night and lunar orientated rather than day and solar, with night as the time of origins and beginnings, the key phase by which all others were counted. In folklore certain female figures are associated symbolically with both sun and moon, while in early Irish sources Saint Bride, derived from the pagan goddess Bride, Brigit (Brighid) or Briggidda, seems to be a 'solar' goddess, as her attributes are light, inspiration and the skills associated with fire such as metal-working and therapy. There is no proof, however, that she was identified with the physical sun, but rather with the inner healing and inspiring fire of vital energy.

One of the most widespread Celtic gods is Bel or Belenos, who represented the power of light and has many solar attributes. In both Gaul and Britain during the

Celtic gods and goddesses appear in Three Worlds or aspects; the pattern of Three Worlds is found in magic, mythology and ancient tradition worldwide. The Three Worlds may be classified as follows:

The Classical Pattern (Found in later Celtic, classical and early Christian symbolism):
1 The Stellar World: consists of the Constellations
2 The Solar World: consists of the Sun and Planets
3 The Lunar World: consists of the Moon and Earth.

In early Christian tradition, and Celtic Christianity, the first World was the realm of Universal Being and the Four Powers and Archangels; the second World was the realm of the Son of Light, or Christ, and the redeeming Angels; the third World was the realm of lesser spirits, humans and all other created entities.

The Chthonic Pattern (Found in primal mythology and magical traditions, and inherent in Celtic religion):
1 *Sky World* contains the gods and goddesses related to major cycles and patterns visible above the horizon, symbolised by Sun, Moon, Stars; is the realm of highest seership or spirit flight as practised in Druidic or shamanistic magic
2 *Earth World* contains humans, animals and other entities, including gods and goddesses relating to the forces of nature and the power of the Land; contains within itself a reflection of the Three Worlds, the *Three Zones* (see figure):

A The upper zone contains the forces of weather, augury through bird flight, and the typical or general range of magical seership or spirit flight as practised in Druidic and shamanistic magic

B The middle zone contains the Four Directions of East, South, West and North, and is the realm of humans, animals and plants, and the general territory of consciousness in humanity; it is a model or prototype for the Sacred Land, which becomes defined geographically or tribally in various territories or locations

C The lower zone taps into the Underworld, and contains sacred springs, wells, lakes, caves, burial mounds and chambers; this is the realm of fairies, elder gods and goddesses, and the dimension of dark prophetic Druidic or shamanistic magic, relating to the Crone or Dark Goddess

3 *Underworld* contains ancestral beings, ex-humans, gods, goddesses and other entities controlling the originative and mysterious energies of death, life and rebirth. The Underworld is linked harmonically to the stars, and certain Underworld gods and goddesses also have a stellar role.

Roman period this god was identified with Apollo. But we should be very cautious not to identify inevitably a god of light or beauty with actual worship of the physical sun. It seems more likely that the sun and moon were regarded as cosmic expressions, physical models, of the same forces that empowered the forms of god and goddess. This viewpoint has been retained in magical arts and mystical disciplines worldwide into the present day. Our illustration of the Three Worlds (Figure B) shows how a god or goddess might have a triple expression, role or powers, manifesting and acting in different ways in each world, yet remaining essentially unchanged.

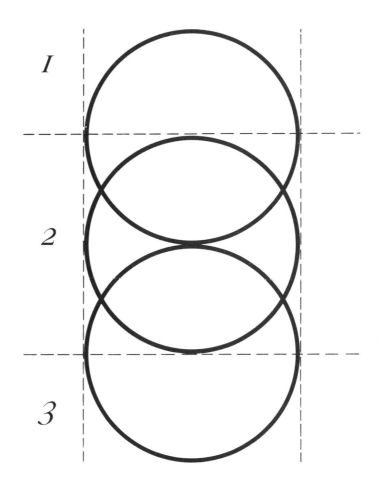

Totem Animals

As with solar worship, so with animals. Victorian scholars tended to assume that the Celts *worshipped* animals. This is a very simplistic and inadequate conclusion. Animals represented, by association, certain powers or deities. Thus each god or goddess has a totem animal, a creature that represents power in operation. This relationship of animals and deities builds into a complex harmonic alphabet of energies and religious or magical practices. The same alphabetic or cyclical structure was applied to trees and other plants. Indeed, it was ultimately the living language of the land, for it included places, people, animals, plants and all the visible and invisible entities of nature. Each land had a sacred centre, from which all forces spiralled outwards. Many of the great Celtic legends, including those of Merlin and the god-child Mabon, involve sequences of animals, trees and other entities which lead back to the sacred centre or the divine being. This harmonic world-view is the key to understanding Celtic myth and legend.

Typical totem animals are the boar, the wolf, the crow, the bear, the bull, the horse, the serpent, the ram, the stag. Each of these is found in both inscription and legend associated with certain gods, goddesses, magicians and heroes.

ROLE OF TOTEM ANIMALS IN MYTH AND WORSHIP

It is often assumed that animals were, and still are, worshipped in primal societies. The actuality is more complex; so complex in many cases that we may not produce a simple summary. Modern primitive peoples, for example, may appear to worship or attach beliefs to the animals of their environment, but attributes and beliefs can be more complex than those that would reasonably develop from the behaviour or habits of the creatures themselves. When we consider the sacred animals of the ancient Celts, we encounter a similar problem, for they were expressions of an entire magical religion and cosmology, and could be interpreted upon varying levels.

Animals were often attached to specific gods and goddesses, and though this seems to suggest layers of conceptual development from primitive animal worship to expression of animal powers in anthropomorphic images, such a reduction is insufficient. There is a quite false 'evolutionary' picture that is often applied to myth, legend and religion: we see first our ignorant ancestors worshipping plants and animals; then we find that the same forces, perhaps refined by a growing understanding of the seasons, are shown as gods and goddesses,

The King Stone from the megalithic ritual complex of the Rollright Stones, Oxfordshire. Such stones are traditionally associated with kingship, sacrifice and the sacred quality of the land. A stone was the totem of kingship in Ireland and Scotland and regarded with such reverence that the king stone of Scone was stolen from medieval Scotland by the invading English, and now resides in Westminster Abbey.

who still have attendant animals; next we find a hierarchical pantheon developing, and finally we reach monotheism with all subsidiary elements disposed of in favour of a single (usually male) deity. Fortunately this absurd picture is now being replaced by a more perceptive and open-minded approach to pre-Christian religion.

But much of the interpretative literature on Celtic religion is still heavily influenced, albeit unconsciously, by Christian dogma, and further confused by the fusion of dogma with a superficially satisfying theory of religious evolution. By such means are the vitality and living qualities removed from Celtic mythology and magic, leaving us further than ever from the worship, philosophy, metaphysics and magic of the people themselves.

RELATIONSHIP BETWEEN ANIMALS AND DEITIES

One way of approaching the subtle relationship between land, animals, people and divinities that permeated Celtic culture would be to work from a principle of *unity*. In other words, the world-view of the Celts was a unified one in which all parts were harmonically enfolded within one another.

Thus we might consider an animal such as the pig, one of the most sacred of Celtic animals, to represent certain energies of the land. These energies, embodied within the animal, were thus set in motion, partaking of both animal and land. The animal acted as a bridging creature between worlds . . . thus the pig was a creature of both the Underworld and the human world, because of its associations with fertility, plenty, food and multiple birth. The animal in turn was associated with a divinity . . . in the case of the pig with a mother goddess (known in Welsh tradition as Cerridwen, the Sow), and with certain heroes, kings, gods and magicians, who were associated with the pig through their dedication or service to the Goddess. We shall return to this concept frequently as we discuss Celtic myth and magical symbolism[24].

While the pig represents certain energies or forces active within the animal or natural world, the Goddess was a *higher form* of such forces. She ruled many worlds and beings, and embodied certain spiritual qualities over and above the elemental or natural qualities found in her totem animal. Thus an animal reveals through its attributes certain key energies, while the deity associated with the animal reveals the wisdom and knowledge required to mediate or use such energies, yet still incorporates those energies.

A short summary of the major Celtic totem animals and their divinities is useful before we proceed further into characteristics of the gods and goddesses themselves, but the following is by no means a detailed study, for totem animals in Celtic mythology and magic would fill a separate book in their own right.

The Boar or Pig is found both in extensive tradition and in archaeological evidence. Pork, and specifically boar's flesh, is frequently found as the magical Otherworld food; pork joints were buried in the lavishly equipped graves of Celtic chieftains to provide for the Otherworldly feast. The Irish prophetic ritual of *Imbis Forosnai* involved eating the flesh of a red pig, a cat or a dog. Red is the colour of the Otherworld in Celtic tradition, and is associated with the Great Goddess in the ritual colours of red, black, and white, which are still found today in ceremonial masks such as the Padstow Hobby Horse in Cornwall.

Sheela-na-Gig, carved on Kilpeck Church, Herefordshire. This image may have represented a female demon to the medieval monastic, but is derived from a Celtic goddess of sexuality, life and death.

The Well of Eternal Youth, on the sacred island of Iona, Scotland. Holy wells and springs frequently pre-date their Christian associations or saints, and were especially revered by the Celts both before and during the Christian era. Folklore and customs are still attached to holy wells today in Celtic regions.

Boars appear on Romano–Celtic coins and in early relief carvings. The boar was also a favourite animal to use as a terminal for the Celtic military trumpet, the squealing of the enraged boar being a sign of valour and an unstoppable charge.

A statue of Diana riding upon a boar reveals a typical fusion of classical and Celtic myth: Diana is the Romanized expression of the ancient native goddess associated with the hunt, powers of birth and death, and the pig. Inscriptions are known to Moccus, which simply means 'pig': the word is found again over a thousand years after the Roman empire had collapsed, when a magical etymology of *moch* or pig is given in the *Mabinogion*, where the pig appears as a magical animal in association with the magician Math.

So they went unto Math the Son of Mathonwy. 'Lord' said Gwydion, 'I have heard that there have appeared in the South some beasts such as were never known in this island before.' 'What are they called?' asked Math. 'Pigs, lord.' 'And what kind of animals are they?' 'They are small animals, and their flesh is better than the flesh of oxen.' 'They are small then?' 'Yes, and they change their names . . . swine are they now called!' 'And who owneth them?' 'Pryderi the son of Pwyll; they were sent to him from Annwn, by Arawn the king of Annwn.' . . . 'And by what means may they be obtained from him?' 'I will go, lord, as one of twelve, in the guise of bards, to seek the swine.' 'It may be that he will refuse you,' said Math; 'I will not come back without the swine,' replied Gwydion. 'Gladly,' said Math, 'go thou forward.'

(From 'Math, Song of Mathonwy', *The Mabinogion* translated by Lady Charlotte Guest)

51

In the same collection of tales we find that the hunting of a giant Boar is a major heroic task undertaken by King Arthur and his men . . . leading ultimately to the liberation of the god-child Mabon. The prophet Merlin is also associated with a pig in an old Welsh poem, where he addresses his pet pig. We may presume that this theme derives from a much earlier motif in which the pig was the totem animal of a god or goddess. In Ireland pigs were said to have been introduced by the Tuatha De Danann (see page 130).

The old British god Bladud, who presides over the hot springs and temple of Aquae Sulis (Bath, England) is also associated with the pig, in a curious traditional tale first printed in the seventeenth or eighteenth century, but clearly deriving from local folk tradition. In this story (from *Pierce's Memoirs* of 1697) the leprous prince is first exiled, as no blemished king could rule, then upon his clandestine return to Britain from Greece is led to his cure in the hot springs by a herd of swine, to which he had become keeper. Upon being cured, he returned to claim his rightful place as prince, and becoming king dedicated a temple to Minerva at the springs, which may still be seen to this day[25].

This early portion of the Bladud legend is not found in the medieval chronicles, but Geoffrey of Monmouth (*History of the Kings of Britain*), writing in the twelfth century, introduces Bladud as the founder of the hot springs and temple, and a great master of Druidic arts including necromancy and magical flight. He also makes Bladud an ancestor of King Arthur, possibly drawing upon Welsh or Breton bardic tradition to this effect. Bladud is again mentioned in the *Vita Merlini* by Geoffrey, as a guardian of therapeutic springs and wells.

As an interesting aside relating to King Bladud, the pig and the Underworld, we find that the cosmology of the *Vita Merlini* seems to place Bladud and the hot springs of Bath in the centre of the land of Britain, which in turn is placed in the centre of the world, providing a gateway to the mysterious Otherworld[26].

From such evidence we may conclude that the pig was closely involved with Underworld or transformative powers; it was the totem beast of the Goddess of life, death and therapy who permeated the ancient world in various forms. Furthermore, both in the *Mabinogion* and the Bladud episode, we find the pig or boar as a psychopomp, leading a hero or heroes to their destiny and fulfilment, verifying kingship, and in the event of failure, to death and destruction.

The Bear is another animal with symbolic attributes that have survived well into the historical period. The bear was still associated as a heraldic animal with the old Stewart family of Traquair in Scotland as late as the eighteenth century, as a sign of kingship. Even at this late stage we find such symbolism, reminiscent of the possible relationship between King Arthur and the bear, commented upon by various writers. Connections have been suggested between Arthur, the bear, and the constellation of Arcturus, the Great Bear of the north. We may indeed have in this tenuous connection a motif that extends back to the stellar mythology of very early Celtic culture. The root word *ar* may also mean 'ploughed land', suggesting connections between Arthur and the constellation of the Plough.

The old Celtic word for bear was *artos*: this is found incorporated into various place names such as Artobranus and Artodunum, of which there are over two hundred variants known in Gaul. The name Arthgen/Artogenus is known from the Roman period, simply meaning 'son of the bear', or perhaps 'son of the Bear

God'. The goddesses Artio and Andarta were Bear Goddesses, and there is a classical parallel in the Greek goddess Artemis, who could take the form of a bear. An image of a Bear Goddess offering fruit to a bear was found at Berne, bearing the inscription *Deae Artioni Licinia Sabinilla*. In an Irish context, stone figures of bears from the pagan Celtic period were found during the rebuilding of Armagh Cathedral in 1840.

The Bull features strongly in the creation mythology of Ireland, and two bulls form the foundation of the vast heroic and magical epic of the *Tain Bo Cuilange* in which the hero Cuchulainn plays an important role. Certain ritual practices associated with bulls are found all over the Western world, and one of the famous seership rituals of the Druids involved being wrapped in the hide of a freshly slain bull. This seems to have parallels with similar ceremonies practised by American Indians.

Bulls have been found featured on coins, as statuettes, and in relief carving in eastern and central Gaul, and in both Scotland and England. An impressive

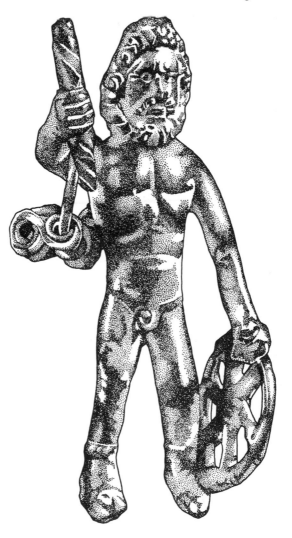

Romano–Celtic image of Taranis, identified with Jupiter. He carries a wheel and a thunderbolt.

53

Romano–Celtic carving found in Paris shows a mythic scene connected with the bull that may be interpreted in a number of different ways. An inscription (*Tarvos Trigaranos* means the bull with three cranes) underpins the visual image of the god Esus cutting down a tree, which has its branches reaching over the representation of the bull. A similar image from Trier shows a male figure cutting down a tree, and in the branches can be seen three cranes and the head of a bull (see illustration on page 11). The god (Esus), bull, crane and tree are all major elements of Western pagan religion and magic, found extensively in classical and Celtic mythology. Even though it is not possible to define the bull-with-three-cranes in a full mythological context, they are clearly part of a Celtic tradition similar to that found in the Irish sagas.

The ritual slaying, flaying and eating of a bull were a central part of a prophetic ceremony in ancient Ireland, in which Druids entered a sacred sleep to gain a vision of the future king; it seems likely that the tree-cutting and bull-with-three-cranes scenes are connected to the sacrificial kingship that underpinned Celtic culture from the earliest period.

The Horse or Mare is best known through the worship of the goddess Epona, an eponymous deity known in Britain and Gaul. Her British and Irish equivalents are Rhiannon (Wales) and Macha and Etain (Ireland).

It seems likely that the famous White Horse and Uffington Castle (in Berkshire, England) are constructs of the Belgae, who worshipped Epona. The horse goddess appears also in the *Mabinogion* in the form of Rhiannon, deriving from Rig Antona or Great High Queen. In her tale the power and fertility of the horse, and its connection to the sacred kingship, are found in a confused and shadowy form. Interestingly, when we consider the motif of the bull and three cranes described above, Rhiannon, the horse goddess, is also associated with birds, whose songs could awaken the dead and lull the living to sleep.

Giraldus Cambrensis tells us, in a famous scene from his account of medieval Ireland, *Topographia Hibernica*, that a tribal king was ritually married to a mare. This pagan folk custom derives from the earlier worship of the Great Goddess and her totem creature, the horse.

The Serpent is one of the important Underworld or magical animals found in Celtic tradition. The late legends of St Patrick banishing serpents from Ireland may relate to pagan worship of the serpent. Certainly the ram-headed serpent was associated with the god Cernunnos, the Lord of the Underworld, or Lord of Animals. Serpents are frequently found on torcs, the sacred neck ornament of Celtic kings and divinities; such serpents may also have a ram's head. The dramatic relief carving of a Celtic god, dating from the Romano–Celtic temple of Aquae Sulis, seems to have a huge double-headed torc around his neck. Sometimes deities offer torcs to serpents; while in early Irish graves from the Bronze Age immense golden torcs have been found, long enough to wrap around an entire body, or perhaps around a sacred stone.

The Stag is associated with Cernunnos, the horned god found in Gaulish inscriptions and in many British legends and place names with the element 'Cerne'. He is especially associated with the lordship of horned and hoofed animals, and with the 'wild hunt' in which spirits of the dead were carried to the

Otherworld. The Stag also features as an important animal in the Merlin legends, which give so many insights into Celtic mythology and magic, for in the *Vita Merlini* Merlin becomes Lord of the Animals, complete with horns and vast herd of goats and stags. This medieval tale is clearly a reworking of pagan tradition, all the more remarkable for its persistence in bardic lore as late as the twelfth century[26].

St Augustine, of course, had grandly issued strict instructions that people were not to indulge in 'that most filthy habit of dressing up as a stag' but his injunction was ignored more often than obeyed. Even today ceremonial animals

Bronze of Sucellus, the 'Good Striker', from Prémeaux. This mallet-wielding Romano–Celtic god may be identified with the Daghdha, the club-wielding father god of the Irish Celts.

such as hobby-horses are still found in folk rituals in Britain and Europe, often connected to a death and resurrection ceremony.

ANIMALS AND TRIBAL OR PERSONAL TABOOS

It seems very likely that specific tribes, families and individuals were connected magically to certain animals. The Irish hero Cuchulainn was not allowed to eat the flesh of a dog or hound, his totem beast. His ultimate defeat is partly as a result of being forced into a situation where he has to take a mouthful of dog's flesh. Certain animals were long considered unlucky to eat or kill, or even to see, and such folklore reflects a primal situation in which the animals, land and people were held to have a harmonic resonance with one another.

TOTEMISM

Power was shown on animal images by unusual combinations: three horns, ram-headed serpents. This is extended to the animal attributes given to anthropomorphic images, the prime example being that of the Lord of the Animals, Cernunnos, who appears with antlers growing from his head.

On a collective tribal level, links to sacred animals and plants were retained well into the modern historical period. In Scotland, for example, the Stewart clan confederacy had the cat as a totem animal, and this totem covered the confederacy of a number of tribes, clans and families. In ancient Celtic culture totems were worn on helmets, as trumpet and arms decorations, and possibly as tattoos: we have numerous examples of such use of animals on Celtic artifacts generally.

The *geas* or taboo concerning certain animals and plants is well known in Celtic legend and folklore; we have mentioned Cuchulainn and his totem dog or hound, but such totemism appears as late as the sixteenth century, when Mary Queen of Scots chose the hare as her emblem. This animal had long been superstitiously associated with witchcraft, through its sacred history within ancient Celtic religion. The warrior queen Boudicca, in the first century AD, may have had the hare as her totem animal – she released a hare that she had kept concealed in her cloak to inspire tribal warfare against the Romans.

Julius Caesar makes some comments which imply totem or animal taboos; certain British tribes considered eating the hare, goose and other fowl as sacrilegious or unlawful, though they kept such creatures among themselves. We have noticed that many Celtic names are associated with animals, from the earliest Romano–Celtic inscriptions to late legends preserved in medieval manuscripts.

MARRIAGE AND SUCCESSION

Associated with the clan taboos and totems is a very ancient system of matrilinear succession, which persisted in Scotland well into the medieval period and beyond. Exogamic marriages were the rule in early Celtic culture, and succession was often retained through the sister–son rather than by direct linear inheritance. Indeed, the entire concept of inheritance, patrilinear descent and primogeniture was introduced into Scottish noble families only as late as the eleventh and twelfth centuries. The old Celtic social patterns are reflected by mythic patterns that were preserved in both literature and oral tradition long after their significance had been forgotten or replaced by other customs. Many of the curiosities of Arthurian legends, for example, may be explained by the systems mentioned above.

Mother Goddesses

It is often assumed that the mother goddesses of the ancient world were large, ample, friendly fertility figures. This is seldom true. The great goddesses of pagan religion were often terrifying and mysterious beings, and those of the Celts seem partiularly fierce to the modern mind, cushioned as we are by centuries of male-dominated state religion, and then blandished by several generations of materialism. It would be insufficient, however, to assume that because Celtic goddesses were often daunting with terrible powers over life, death and fate, that they are an unfortunate legacy from the vicious primitive past. In many ways the attributes of ancient feminine powers or archetypes reveal a deep insight into reality, not merely the reality of nature and human life relating to the land, but the reality of the human mind, imagination and spirit.

Awesome goddesses like the Irish Morrigan, who often appears in triple form, are not stereotypical seekers after blood and battle, but reveal an inherent unity of life and death: the Morrigan controls both death and sexuality, and may appear as an alluring but deadly maiden or a screaming hag in early tales; hence she takes in order to give.

This may seem superficially similar to certain modern psychological theories, but it runs far deeper, for it relates not only to the surface of the human psyche, but to the collective imagination, and to vital relationships between people and the land. Nothing can live without death: in this context it is significant to find that Celts counted time not by days, but by nights, and made their calendars (such as the famous Coligny calendar) not by the sun but by the moon. The term *fortnight* is still found in the English language, and may be a relic from the ancient habit of counting time by nights . . . a fourteen-night or half of the lunar cycle.

Put more simply, we must understand and accept the taking powers in life in order to obtain the benefit of the giving powers. This cyclical pattern is most noticeable in communities which live close to the land, be they hunters or farmers (and the Celts were both, though they seem to have originated as nomadic or semi-nomadic peoples). One of the greatest of Celtic gods, who was both the son and the consort of the Mother at different phases of the cycle, was the Hunter God, also known as Cernunnos from various figures and inscriptions. He controlled the culling, purifying and health of the herds, and seems to have been particularly associated with deer, though in Irish tradition there are semi-divine cowherds, while in the late medieval *Mabinogion* we find Cernunnos appearing as a dark powerful figure who is Lord of All Animals.

'Sleep here tonight, and in the morning arise early, and take the road upwards through the valley until thou reachest the wood. A little way within the wood thou wilt meet with a road branching off to the right, by which thou must proceed, until thou comest to a large sheltered glade with a mound in the centre. And thou wilt see a black man of great stature on the top of the mound. He is not smaller in size than two men of this world. He has but one foot, and one eye in the middle of his forehead. And he has a club of iron, and it is certain that there are no two men in the world who would not find their burden in that club. And he is not a comely man, but on the contrary he is exceedingly ill favoured; and he is the woodward of that wood. And thou wilt see a thousand wild animals grazing all around him. Inquire of him the way out of the glade, and he will reply to thee briefly, and will point out the road by which thou shalt find thy quest.'

And long seemed that night to me. And the next morning I arose and equipped myself, and mounted my horse, and proceeded straight through the valley to that wood. And I followed the cross-road which the man had pointed out to me till at length I arrived at the glade. And there was I three times more astonished at the number of wild animals that I beheld than he had said I should be! And the great black man was there, sitting upon the top of the mound. Huge of stature was he, and I found him to

Hercules or Ogmios, from High Rochester, Northumberland, England.

59

exceed by far the description that had been given me of him. As for the iron club which it would have been a heavy weight for four warriors to lift, yet it was in the black man's hand. And he only spoke to me in answer to my questions.

Then I asked him what power he had over those animals. 'I will show thee, little man,' said he. And he took his club in his hand, and with it he struck a stag so great a blow that it brayed vehemently, and at the braying all the animals came together, as numerous as the stars in the sky, so that it was difficult for me to find room in the glade to stand among them. There were serpents and dragons and divers sorts of animals. And the great black man looked at them, and bade them go and feed, and they bowed their heads, and did him homage as vassals to their lord.

(From 'The Lady of the Fountain', The Mabinogion,
translated by Lady Charlotte Guest)

This dark son of the Mother is balanced by a light son, Mabon the divine child of Light, the Celtic Apollo, whom we shall consider in some detail in a later chapter. The implication of twin brothers, or dark and light aspects of one

---

FIGURE C
THE TRIPLE GODDESS, AND THE FOURFOLD CYCLE

I =	Maiden	
II =	Mother	
III =	Crone	
1	East/Spring/Air/Dawn/Beginning	
2	South/Summer/Fire/Noon/Increasing	
3	West/Autumn/Water/Evening/Maturing	
4	North/Winter/Earth/Night/Destroying	

The Triad or Triangle of the Goddess rotates around the Fourfold Cycle, through the Four Seasons and Elements.

divinity, should not be confused with later repressive concepts such as 'God and the Devil'; the polarity of pagan gods and goddesses was of positive and negative, summer and winter, with each aspect having, in turn, its own inherent positive and negative qualities. In Irish legend we find that battles between races described in the *Book of Invasions* give each mythical race a polarized role as they are replaced by the next. Thus the gods and beings of the old order tend to be equated with dark or negative forces by those of the new, but likewise the older gods and goddesses are essential to the foundations and continuation of the world, and are never entirely disposed of (see page 126).

TRIPLE GODDESSES

Celtic goddesses frequently are shown or described in triple form. The Celts used a triple cycle for the seasons and for many magical patterns within religion. This was further enhanced by a fourfold cycle, which is identical in many ways with the classical cycle of the Four Elements, Four Seasons, Four Ages, Four Directions, or the Wheel of Life, which feature in philosophical and metaphysical literature and traditions from ancient Greek writers to the Renaissance and on into the nineteenth- and twentieth-century magical treatises and systems of initiation and enlightenment[27] (see Figure A).

The triplication of pagan goddesses was summarized by the late Robert Graves

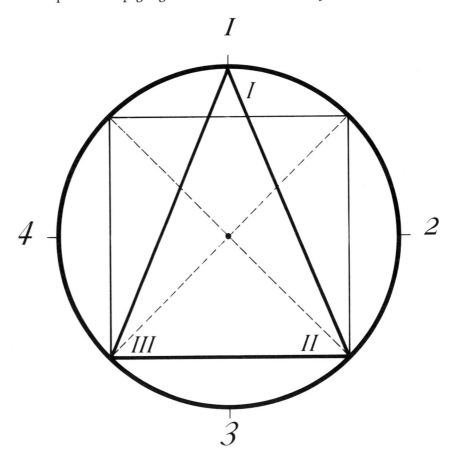

The Goddess and the Four Directions

into a cycle of Maiden, Mother and Crone. Graves drew extensively upon his classical education, and upon a rare source book, *Celtic Researches* by Edward Davis, published by subscription in 1804. The concept of triplicity might also be expressed as Virginity, Fertility and Death, or Beginning, Increasing, Destroying. But when we express the triplicity thus, we are using an order that might not have seemed correct to the ancient Celts: they would have used Crone, Maiden, Mother, or Destroyer, Beginner, Increaser, or Death, Birth, Fruitfulness. Before light, darkness, and before day, night.

This nocturnal lunar and stellar emphasis tends to contradict comfortable rationalizations about seasonal gods and solar cycles. We are frequently told, for example, that the four great Celtic festivals (Samhain, Imbolc, Beltane and Lughnasadh) were markers of the solar year, with fires lit at Beltane or Mayday to mark the return of the sun. The festivals of May and November, however, mark the setting and rising of the Pleiades, a small group of stars in the constellation of Taurus. The appearance and disappearance of this star group is observed by rituals all over the world, and we find that the Pleiades play an obscure but important part in Celtic tradition, related to goddesses, as they do in classical myth. Each of the Pleiades is allocated a goddess, and these act as matrices, according to esoteric teaching traditions, for the dynamic forces of the Seven Planets. We do not know if this esoteric tradition was originally employed by the pagan Celts, but the Pleiades certainly acted as stellar markers of great significance in the Celtic year.

Triple goddesses are not exclusively defined by the triple cycle mentioned above, though it does make a good general pattern for our understanding of ancient goddesses, and suggests why they often appeared in triple or multiple partnership at ancient sites. In certain cases we find classical and legendary references to a tripled triplicity, a ninefold sequence or presentation of god-

desses; a sacred island in the River Seine was said to be the sanctuary of nine priestesses, while the Druidic priestess or goddess Morgen ruled the Fortunate Isles with her nine sisters[28]. Such records are echoes of multiple ninefold goddesses, percolating through into early literary traditions.

THE GIVING GODDESS

Although the Celts had no straightforward goddess of love, such as the classical Venus or Aphrodite, they seem to have worshipped a nature goddess, a type of flower and fruit divinity, often portrayed as a beautiful and desirable young woman. In the *Mabinogion*, Llew is given a flower maiden wife, Blodeuwedd, by the great magician Math (see Appendix), while in the medieval *Vita Merlini* Merlin is married to a flower maiden called Guendoloena. Both of these figures appear relatively late in literature, and seem to be related to the Arthurian figure of Guenevere. It is possible that Guendoloena in the *Vita*, who was divorced by Merlin, is an immediate forerunner of the unfortunate queen Guenevere found in the Arthurian legends that were soon to follow.

The *Vita Merlini*, by Geoffrey of Monmouth, was written around 1150 and, like his *History of the British Kings* and *Prophecies of Merlin*, heralded the opening of a flood tide of medieval Arthurian literature, developed from Celtic oral tales into an abundant outpouring of written works. We shall return to the Merlin tradition when we consider Mabon, the Celtic divine child, for it to this realm that Merlin truly belongs, rather than as the stereotypical wise old man of Victorian and modern fiction.

In the Temple of Aquae Sulis we find that the dark prophetic and curse-empowering goddess Sulis was combined or alternated with the Roman culture goddess, the virginal Minerva. This is merely an example of the presence of Crone and Maiden in one sacred site. The figure of Minerva is often found in a Celtic context, for she replaced a native sister or virgin deity, possibly the goddess Brid or Brigantia, who later was known as Brigid or Bride, and then Saint Bride.

The Virgin goddess, or Sister or Maiden, closely related to the Greek Athena, inspired and enabled development of culture, and in this role acted as patroness of heroes in wondrous deeds, and often as both healer and warrior. Is she therefore a goddess of giving or of taking? In some ways she acts as the bridge between the Crone and the Mother ... reminding us again that the order of priority was always crone, maiden, mother.

Bronze scabbard from Co. Antrim, Ireland.

Celtic Goddesses

Celtic goddesses, like the gods, are stark and functional. In common with all genuine god-forms worldwide, regardless of religion, the ancient Celtic deities represented powers, aspects of creative and destructive energy at work. Celtic goddesses may seem, at first, savage and primal to the modern mind . . . but such a reaction is the product of our long, unfortunate conditioning to a monosexual political religion. There is a coy notion, frequently applied to the classical Greek goddesses, and certainly found in modern imaginative fiction, that female deities need to be inflated stereotypes of standard 'femininity'. When we examine the reality of Celtic goddesses, nothing could be further from the truth.

The fundamental root of Celtic goddess imagery and worship is this: the goddess is an embodiment of the forces of the sacred land. This sacred land may be a region or locality of specific topographical location, it may be the territory of a family or tribe, and in higher forms it may be the planet, the solar system or a pattern of stars.

The cult of the Mother Goddess is pre-Celtic, and played a major role in the megalithic culture which built so many vast stone and earth ritual structures the length and breadth of Britain and western Europe. The Celts, in common with all European people, were also worshippers of a mother goddess, and as they moved further west, absorbed and regenerated many of the ritual and religious elements of the indigenous people. In Ireland we find that the *Tuatha De Danann* were, literally translated, the Children of the Goddess Danu, in the sense of a tribe or family that held the goddess to be their supreme divine Mother.

It may also be significant that Donn, who dwells in a mysterious island to the west, is said to be the (male) primal ancestor, who summons the spirits of mortals to his realm. In Wales the Celtic deities, defined as the legendary people of the *Mabinogion* and other traditional tales, were the children or tribe of Don, showing that the nomenclature of the mythology was, in certain cases, widespread. The same name occurs in Ireland in the form of Anu, described in *Cormac's Glossary* as 'the Mother of the deities of Ireland'. One of the controversial Ogham inscriptions found on the eastern seaboard of the USA is to the goddess Byanu, and if this is indeed a genuine Celtic inscription it shows that the Goddess travelled very far indeed with her worshippers.

In various parts of Britain we find the Goddess referred to merely as Modron, which means 'mother'. This misleadingly simple term suggests that the cult of the Mother Goddess was widespread, for, regardless of her local names, she was

The Lord of Light destroys Chaos. Lugh, the Irish god of Light, casts his deadly slingshot at his grandfather Balor, King of the Fomorians. The myth describes a great battle, in which a new order of gods and goddesses take over from the primal beings of chaotic energy, and bring skill and order to the Sacred Land.

known everywhere as Modron, just as her divine child was known as Mabon, which simply means 'son'.

The goddess of Sovereignty, who mediates and represents the energies of the land, is well known in Irish mythological tradition, often in triple form. The incoming Gaels, the first humans, but the last race, to arrive in Ireland, wooed the Goddess in her aspects of Banbha, Fodla and Eriu (see page 134). This same figure appears in the enigmatic *Prophecies of Merlin* as a maiden who purifies the land, so becoming mature and growing to giant stature, encompassing the north and south of Britain, which she holds in either hand.

Three springs shall break forth in the city of Winchester, whose rivers shall divide the island [of Britain] into three parts. Whoever shall drink of the first spring shall enjoy long life and never be afflicted with sickness. Whoever shall drink of the second, shall die of hunger, and paleness and horror shall be seen upon his countenance.

Whoever shall drink of the third spring shall be surprised by sudden death, neither shall his body be possible to bury. Those that seek to escape so voracious a death will endeavour to hide it with several coverings, but whatever bulk shall be laid upon it shall be transformed into another substance. For earth shall be turned to stones, stones into water, [water into wood?], wood into ashes, ashes into water when they are cast over such a body.

And a maiden shall be sent from the City within the Hoary Forest, to administer a cure. Once she has practised her oracular arts, she shall dry up the noxious fountains by breathing upon them. Afterwards, as soon as she has refreshed herself with the wholesome spring, she shall bear in her right hand the forests of Caledon [Scotland], and in her left, the buttressed forts of London.

Wherever she shall go, she shall make sulphurous steps, which shall smoke with a double flame. That smoke shall rouse up the Ruteni ['swift ones'; also a Celtic tribal name] and shall make food for the inhabitants of the deep sea. Tears of compassion will overflow her eyes, and she shall fill the island with dreadful cries.

She shall be killed by a hart with ten branches, four of which shall bear golden diadems; but the other six shall be turned into horns of oxen, whose hideous bellowings shall arouse the three islands of Britain.

(From *The Prophecies of Merlin*, translated by J. A. Giles.
For a detailed commentary see *The Prophetic Vision of Merlin*
by R. J. Stewart, Arkana, 1986)

In many Celtic legends, woman has a major role, while her consort is secondary. This status is derived from the ancient religion, in which goddesses were considered more powerful than gods, and from a matriarchal phase of Celtic culture. We find it reflected in the famous character of Queen Medbh, the immensely powerful protagonist of the *Tain Bo Cuailnge* or 'Cattle Raid of Cooley'. Medbh changes her lovers frequently, because men were secondary to her as a queen, the epitome of Sovereignty.

We know that the king was wedded to the land and, if he failed, the land was likely to fail; this theme, far from showing how important the king might have been, actually shows how easily replaceable he was; the land endures, but kings come and go according to patterns of good and ill.

In 'The Cattle Raid of Cooley', we find the great Ulster hero Cuchulainn in conflict with the Morrigan, and failing to recognize her supremacy. Eventually this is his undoing, for it is the goddess who forces him to break his *geas* or magical obligation, thus weakening his previously invincible energies and skills. In one of the mythical and humorous encounters between Cuchulainn and

The Flower Maiden. Blodeuwedd, the Welsh Flower-Bride, formed of blossoms by the magicians Gwydion and Math. She betrayed her intended husband, Llew, and caused him to undergo the Three-fold Death at the hands of her lover, the hunter Gronw Pebr. Gwydion later transformed her into an owl, the night bird with a 'flower face'.

OVERLEAF LEFT: *The Lord of the Animals.* Cernunnos, 'Horned One', whose images are found in Romano–Celtic worship sites, and whose role as hunter and animal god is preserved in Celtic legend and folklore. He ruled the active forces of life and death, giving and taking, in nature; in Romano–Celtic culture he was associated with wealth and prosperity, due to his role as Guardian of the Gateway to the Underworld where all potential forces and events originated.

OVERLEAF RIGHT: *Lady of Bright Inspiration.* Brighid, Gaelic goddess of smithcraft and metalwork, poetic inspiration and therapy. The ancient *filid* or bards were under her direct inspiration, and in folk tradition she is said to have been the midwife and foster-mother of Jesus. Her primal function is that of fire and illumination; in Romano–Celtic temples she was frequently amalgamated with the goddess Minerva.

Otherworld beings, it is interesting to find that the woman (a thinly disguised goddess) rides in a chariot, while her male consort walks, a sign of inferiority or servitude. Furthermore, she has the right to answer all questions, and a mockery is made of Cuchulainn based upon this ancient supremacy of female over male.

Cuchulainn meets the Morrigan

When Cuchulainn lay asleep in Dun Imrid, he heard a cry sounding out of the North, a cry that was terrible and fearful to his ears. Out of his deep slumber he was aroused so suddenly, that he fell out of his bed upon the ground like a sack, in the eastern part of his house.

He rushed forth without weapons, until he gained the open air, his wife following him with his armour and his garments.

Then Cuchulainn saw Laegh, his charioteer, in a harnessed chariot coming towards him from the North.

'What brings you here?' said Cuchulainn. 'A great cry that I heard sounding across the plain,' answered Laegh.

'From which direction?' said Cuchulainn.

'From the North West,' said Laegh, 'across the great highway that leads to Caill Cuan.'

'Then let us follow that sound,' said Cuchulainn, 'and find the source of it!'

They rode forward as far as Ath de Ferta. When they arrived there, they heard the rattle of a chariot, from the loamy district of Culgaire. They saw before them a chariot harnessed with a chestnut horse. And this horse was a wonder, for it had one leg, and one eye, and one ear, and the pole of the chariot passed right through its body, so that the peg in front met the halter, which passed across its forehead.

Within the chariot sat a fearsome woman, her eyebrows red of colour, and a crimson mantle wrapped about her. This mantle fell behind her between the wheels of the chariot, so that it swept along the ground. Walking beside the chariot was a big strapping man. He also wore a coat of crimson colour, and upon his back he carried a forked staff of white hazelwood. This man drove before him a fine glossy coated cow.

'The cow is not happy at all to be driven along by you!' said Cuchulainn.

'But she does not belong to you! Not to you or any of your gang of warriors,' replied the woman.

'All of the cattle of Ulster are in my own keeping.'

'So . . . you would be a druid and give decisions about the law of cattle ownership? You are taking too much upon yourself, Cuchulainn.'

'How come this woman knows my name? Why is it always her who speaks, when it should be the man who addresses me?' cried Cuchulainn.

'Ah, but you did not speak to the man first, so why should he speak to you?'

'Yes, but when I talk of men's decisions, it is you, woman, who immediately and loudly answer me. Tell me this man's name then, that I might speak to him now!'

'If you would speak with him, you must call him by his true name, which is OOAR GAAETH SKEEOO LOOCHAAIR SKEEOO.'

'Well indeed, the length of that name is truly astonishing! But as this man chooses to remain silent and glum and speak not at all, I demand to know *your* name, woman!' roared Cuchulainn. But it was the man who replied:

'The woman to whom you speak is called FAAEVOOR VEG BEEOOIL COOOMDUIR FOOLT SKENV GAIRFET SKEEO OOATH!'

'You are making a fool of me!' And with this, Cuchulainn made a great leap, right into that fearsome woman's chariot. He placed his two strong feet upon her two shoulders, and put his sharp edged spear against the parting of her flame red hair.

'Do not play with your weapons upon me!'

'Then tell me your true name.'

The Young Son of Light. Mabon or Maponus, the Celtic god of liberation, harmony, unity and music. He may have been one of the most universally worshipped deities in the Celtic world, and was at the centre of the Druidic magical cosmology as the original Being, pre-existent, Son of the Great Mother. He is represented in myth and legend as both a prisoner and a liberator; many other heroic and divine figures are related to Mabon.

OVERLEAF LEFT: *The Hero.* Cuchulainn son of Sualtam, but really the son of Lugh. The great Ulster hero, guardian of the Sacred Land. Like many heroes in ancient myth, he bridges the human and divine, with parents in both worlds. His entire life is set about with magical obligations and portents, and his sole function is to defend his people and their land, even at the expense of his own life.

OVERLEAF RIGHT: *The Lord of Thunder.* Taranis, god of the wheel. One of the powerful Father Gods, associated with forces of change. The Romans associated him with their Jupiter, and with the shadowy Dis Pater, the primal god of the Underworld. His connection to the oak tree and to thunder, both of which were important symbols and entities in Druidism, suggests that he may have been a specifically Druidic father god.

'Get away from me then. I am a female poet and a satirist, and this man is Daire mac Fiachna of Cuailgne. And as for this cow, I carry it off as my reward for a fine poem.'

'Huh! So let us hear this fine poem of yours!'

'Move further off and get away then. Your shaking of that thing over my head will not influence or worry me at all, not in the least.'

Then he moved away from her as she asked, until he was standing right between the two wheels of her chariot. And then she sang to him and sang her fine poem. When the singing stopped Cuchulainn made ready to leap into the chariot again with his spear, but horse, man, chariot, and cow, had all disappeared.

(From *The Cuchulainn Saga*, edited by Eleanor Hull)

One of the major features of Celtic goddesses is a fusion of fertility powers with those of war: this may seem confusing, contradictory or even barbaric to the modern reader, but we need to examine the root of this magical and ultimately metaphysical or poetic fusion of functions and concepts. The goddesses of fertility and war, or sexuality and death, were in effect the Openers and Closers of the Way of Life: the Givers and Takers. These figures, with localized names and functions dependent upon their location within a sacred landscape, were expressions of the One Goddess who presided over all life and death. Thus the apparent conflict between a goddess ruling both fertility and death is only superficial; it would present no problem to the Celt who knew that death comes from life and life from death. This polar cycle of energies, anabolic and catabolic, is central to Celtic mythology, religion and magic.

We find this concept clearly expressed as late as the medieval period in Merlin's vision of the two dragons, one red, one white. A similar theme arises in the *Mabinogion* with the tale of 'Lludd and Llevelys', in which two dragons are imprisoned by a king at the centre of the land to obtain peace for the people.

'And the second plague' [said Llevelys to the king, his brother Lludd] 'that is in thy dominion, behold it is a dragon. And another dragon of a foreign race is fighting with it, and striving to overcome it. And therefore does this dragon make a fearful outcry. And in this wise mayest thou come to know the truth of this. After thou hast returned home, cause the island [of Britain] to be measured in its length and breadth, and in the place where is the exact central point, there cause a pit to be dug, and cause a cauldron full of the best mead that can be brewed to be put in the pit, with a covering of satin over the face of the cauldron. And then, in thine own person, do thou remain there watching, and thou wilt see the dragons fighting in the form of terrifying animals. And at length they will take the form of dragons in the air. And last of all they will fall in the form of two pigs upon the satin covering, and they will sink in, and the covering with them, and they will draw it down to the very bottom of the cauldron. And they will drink up the whole of the mead, and after that they will fall asleep. Thereupon do you immediately fold the covering around them, and bury them in a kist [chest] in the strongest place that thou hast in thy dominions, and hide them deep within the earth. And as long as they shall bide in that strong place, no plague shall come to the Island of Britain from elsewhere.'　(From 'Lludd and Llevelys', *The Mabinogion*, translated by Lady Charlotte Guest)

In Irish legend and in Celtic folklore, the combating and pacifying of serpents is an important theme that harks back to pagan religion. It must be stressed that this is a *pre-Christian* theme, not to be confused with later rationalizations and propagandizing motifs such as that of the Archangel Michael suppressing the great Dragon or Devil. By the Christian era, a long established pagan theme of

Queen of Horses and Fruitfulness. Epona in Celtic inscriptions from Gaul, and Rhiannon in Welsh legend. She is the goddess of horses, and therefore of great power in a horse-based culture such as that of the Celts. In Romano–Celtic images she is associated with corn, fruits and serpents, and as Mare-Goddess she would have been concerned with forces of fertility and nourishment.

OVERLEAF LEFT: *Phantom Queen of Death, Sexuality and Conflict*. The Morrigan, known in Irish legend and mythology as a red-haired goddess of battle and procreation, often appearing in triple form. She combined the threshold energies of life and death, sexuality and conflict in one terrifying goddess. Part of the doom of Cuchulainn was that he did not recognize her when in her presence.

OVERLEAF RIGHT: *The Sea God*. Manannan mac Lir, also called Barinthus. A primal god of the ocean deeps, who is also associated with stellar navigation. In the *Vita Merlini* he ferries the wounded King Arthur, accompanied by the prophet Merlin and the bard Taliesin, to the Otherworld for his cure.

A handsome lad truly was he that stood there, Cuchulainn son of Sualtam was his name. Three colours of hair had he, next to the skin of his head the hair was brown, in the middle it was crimson, on the outside it was like a diadem of gold. Comparable to yellow gold was each glittering long curling splendid beautiful thread of hair, falling freely down between his two shoulders.

About his neck were a hundred tiny links of red gold flashing, with pendants hung from them. His headgear was adorned with a hundred different jewels. On either cheek he had four moles, a yellow, a green, a blue, and a red. In either eye he had seven pupils, sparkling like seven gems. Each of his feet had seven toes, each of his hands had seven fingers. His hands and feet were endowed with the clutching power of hawk's talons and hedgehog's claws.

He wore his gorgeous raiment for great gatherings of chieftains, a fair crimson tunic of five plies all fringed, with a long pin of white silver gold, encased and patterned, shining like a luminous torch, with a brilliance men could not endure to look upon. Next to his skin was a shirt of purest silk, bordered and fringed all around, with gold, silver and white bronze braided up together. His silken shirt came to the upper edge of his russet coloured kilt.

Cuchulainn carried a powerful sacred shield, coloured dark crimson, with a pure white silver rim all around its circumference. At his left side hung a long sharp golden hilted sword. Beside him in his chariot was a lengthy spear, together with a keen aggressive javelin, with a hurling thong and rivets of white bronze. In one of his hands he carried nine severed heads, and in the other hand nine more. He held these heads as emblems of his valour and skill in arms, and at the very sight of him the opposing army shook with terror. (From *The Cuchulainn Saga*, edited by Eleanor Hull)

polarity was altered to represent the dominance of a new religion over the old; the deeper metaphysical or magical levels may have some connectives through to the primal mythology of two dragons within the land, but the overt symbolism is very different.

We may presume that the dragons and serpents of Celtic religion symbolized earth energies, potent forces of the land, which polarized into positive and negative roles. These were originally under the rulership of a goddess, for many of the ancient goddesses were associated with serpents in varying roles. The god, king or hero, who subdues or even slays a serpent in such a context, is acting with the blessing of the goddess as her agent to rebalance energies for the benefit of his people.

[The youthful Merlin has revealed that an underground chamber containing a pool is the cause of collapse of King Vortigern's Tower . . .] Then said he to the king, 'Command the pool to be drained, and at the bottom you will see two hollow stones, and in them two dragons asleep.' The king did not hesitate to believe him, since he had found true what Merlin had said of the pool, and therefore ordered it to be drained. Which done, he found all as Merlin had said, and was possessed of the greatest admiration of him.

And while Vortigern, King of the Britons, was seated upon the bank of the pool that had been drained, there issued forth two dragons, whereof one was white and the other red. And when they drew close to one another, they grappled together in terrible combat, and breathed forth fire. But presently the White Dragon prevailed, and drove the Red to the verge of the pool. But he, grieving to be thus driven, fell fiercely upon the White and forced him to draw back. And whilst they were fighting in this wise, the King bade Ambrosius Merlin declare what this battle of the Dragons portended.

(From *The Prophecies of Merlin*,
translated by J. A. Giles)

HEROES, SERPENTS AND MONSTERS

Although our present context is that of the serpent and goddess, related to the sanctity of the land, it cannot be separated totally from other heroic adventures involving gigantic creatures. The hero in ancient myths formed a bridge between humankind and the gods, or more specifically the goddess of his tribe, locality or land. He was more than a mere man, often having divine parentage on one side of his family, and his role was to enact, embody and empower certain mythical energetic patterns. In the classical world, heroes were worshipped as minor deities, and we find that Celtic heroes such as Cuchulainn or Finn MacCumhaill seem to fulfil such a role. In the British context we find that many of the Arthurian warriors, and of course Arthur himself, mask the images of older gods.

The hero was responsible for the evolutionary or repressive gifts of the gods and goddesses, bringing such forces out into human and environmental conditions. It is in this context that we find the theme of hero and monster running through mythology, and the later repressive aspect of the theme should be considered only in the light of earlier more enduring developments.

In classical myth we have many typical examples of the hero and monster theme:

Bellerophon killed the Chimera, a three-headed monster that breathed forth fire. Like so many heroes, he was aided by Athena (later Minerva), who gave him certain magical gifts including the winged horse Pegasus. On trying to fly into the upper realms of the gods, Bellerophon was unseated when Zeus sent a gadfly to sting Pegasus; he fell to earth to become lame, or in some variants, blind.

Heracles, on the eleventh of his twelve great labours, slew a hundred-headed dragon, which had been set to guard the Golden Apples of the Hesperides. The classical writer Hesiod described the Hesperides, in his *Theogony*, as three sisters, the Daughters of Night, who lived upon an island in the Western Ocean. Such typically Celtic imagery is found in a number of Greek myths. On achieving his task, Heracles gave the golden apples to Athena, who later restored them to the magical garden. The role of Athena/Minerva, who is paralleled in many ways in Celtic mythology by Brigit, is central to many heroic myths, as she was concerned with the development of human potential.

Perseus, Theseus, Jason and others feature in similar tales. The classical elements of the myth are such that a goddess contrives a situation whereby a hero has to fight a seemingly malign creature. She aids him in various ways, then receives from him a token of his victory, which she paradoxically returns to its original location, or returns to its original purpose. A close examination of such myths suggests that the 'monster' is often a dark aspect or totem animal of the goddess herself, and that the true nature of the legend is that of a cycle or spiral of development.

There are numerous parallels in Celtic mythology and legend:

Arthur and his warriors hunt a giant boar, the Twrch Trwyth.

Diancecht, the healer god in Irish lore, slew a giant serpent that threatened and destroyed cattle throughout the land. This reminds us of the legend of Apollo and his connection to therapy and serpents, as he slew the great serpent of the Temple of Delphi.

Finn MacCumhaill destroyed serpents throughout the land of Ireland, each having various attributes of fire and water.

The entire relationship between magical beasts, goddesses and heroes is complex, but certainly related to the health of the land and the well-being of the people therein. By the time it reappears in medieval retelling of Celtic tradition, such as that of Lludd and Llevelys quoted above, the dragons are not necessarily associated with specific heroes, but with the qualities of kingship and the fate of the land. The famous scene involving the usurping King Vortigern and the youthful prophet Merlin (in the *Prophecies of Merlin*) predates the *Mabinogion* in literary history by at least three hundred years, but they are clearly concerned with the same tradition. Indeed, the Merlin episode reads as if it should follow from that of Lludd and Llevelys, for the usurping Vortigern lets loose the dragons enclosed within the hill, said to be Dinas Emrys in the heart of Snowdonia, thus bringing war and ruin upon the land.

Although the dragons in the *Prophecies of Merlin* are rationalized as visions of the Celts and Saxons, we must remember that warring races, contending for the land, were emblematic of forces within the land itself. Thus an overtly racial or political battle is only the outer expression of a spiritual energy or resolution of energies.

WARRIOR GODDESSES

We find warrior goddesses highly placed in Irish tradition; Cuchulainn was taught by the mysterious Scathach upon the Isle of Skye, which to this day is named after her. Her skills were astonishing, and the young warriors of the Celtic lands travelled to her school of martial arts.

Queen Medbh, the instigator of the Cattle Raid of Cooley, was so fearsome that she commanded a vast army of heroes and warriors, and so powerful that her mere presence deprived her opponents of two-thirds of their courage and strength. Such apparently historical or legendary warrior women and queens are manifestations or perhaps thinly disguised variants of the great war goddess, who is usually known in Irish tradition as the Morrigan[29].

THE MORRIGAN

The Morrigan, known from Irish tradition but undoubtedly a Celtic goddess who had expression and images throughout Celtic culture, appears in triple form. Morrigan means 'Phantom Queen', while her other forms are Nemhain and Badhbh meaning 'Frenzy' and 'Crow or Raven'. The mysterious and terrible goddess Andraste, invoked in southern Britain by Queen Boudicca when she revolted against Roman tyranny in the first century AD, is of the same type as the Morrigan.

Traditions of the Washer at the Ford run through Celtic literature and folklore, appearing in instances of the Second Sight and in many traditional tales and ballads as late as the nineteenth or twentieth century. To meet the Washer at the Ford was to meet Death, and to have prevision of the nature of a death, either your own or that of another person. Cuchulainn's death was predicted in this manner, for as he rode to his last battle, he saw a maiden washing clothes and armour at a ford. Just as if he were a stranger whom she did not recognize, she told him that she was washing the armour of one Cuchulainn, son of Sualtam,

who would shortly die. The inevitability and impersonality of the death goddess are frequently emphasized; in imagery deriving from such primal foundations, we find that the goddess of Justice is blind.

HORSE GODDESSES

The goddess Macha is further connected to Emain Macha, the ancient capital city of Ulster, known today as Navan Fort, a prehistoric and possibly ritual or magical structure; she is also associated with Armagh (*Ard Macha*), which was to become the centre for Celtic Christianity. It seems likely that early Christian missionaries deliberately chose to work from a sacred centre of the Goddess, and the relationship between Celtic Druids and early Christian missionaries was by no means as hostile as later propaganda leads us to believe.

A similar situation is found at the sanctuary of the goddess Brid or Brighid, in whose honour a perpetual fire was kept burning; her temple at Kildare in Ireland become one of the great Celtic Christian centres, and still retained the eternal flame tended by maidens (nuns) until it was extinguished at the time of the Reformation.

The goddess Macha is connected to ritual games and festivals, in which contests of skill and arms are linked inseparably to the fertility of the land. One legend of Macha concerns her racing against the royal horses of the king and finally giving birth to twins: we find a similar theme in the story of Rhiannon in the *Mabinogion*.

Rhiannon gives birth to a boy, who is mysteriously abducted while mother and nurses sleep. Fearing revenge, the nurses smear blood and bones from a dog around the sleeping Rhiannon, and declare that she has devoured her child. Judgement is passed upon her for her crime:

> And the penance that was imposed upon her was this, that she should remain in that palace of Narberth until the end of seven years, and that she should sit every day near unto a horse block that was outside the gate. And that she should relate her story to all who should come there if they did not know it already; and that she should offer to carry guests and strangers, if they would permit her, upon her back into the palace. But it rarely happened that any would so permit.
>
> (From 'Pwyll, Prince of Dyfed', *The Mabinogion*, translated by Lady Charlotte Guest)

The concepts of horse goddess, skill and fertility are thus found in Welsh, Irish and Romano–Celtic or Gaelic traditions. The Gaulish horse goddess is known as Epona in ancient inscription, and even to this day the word 'pony' reminds us of her presence.

GODDESSES OF BEAUTY, LONGING AND JOY

Celtic deities, as we have found repeatedly in our examples, tend to have triple aspects or manifestations. The Great Goddess of the ancient world was in triple form, with each of her three aspects being in turn triplicated, giving a Ninefold Goddess. Although the Celtic goddesses do not fit into rigid categories, we have suggested the general relationship of Crone, Mature Woman, and Sister or Maiden. The elusive and shape-changing goddesses will fit into this broad triple division, though each goddess may in herself be triplicated.

A small number of Celtic goddesses, of the Maiden type, fit into the categories of beauty, sorrow and joy. We are perhaps more familiar with this type of deity from popular fiction, romance, poetry and re-telling of Celtic legends, than with the primal and most powerful, fearsome goddesses such as the Morrigan.

Irish legend features certain beautiful maidens of the Otherworld. Although this theme was rationalized in later literature and became typical of 'paradise' where heroic men were rewarded with the love and delights of beautiful women, it is clear from the nature of Celtic goddesses in general that their culture was, in many ways, matriarchal. The later eastern concept of dominant hero and swooning maid is not inherent in Celtic myth. But if we look deeper, we find that the maiden is an aspect of a multiple goddess; as such she draws her hero into the Otherworld, often to set him a task. Such tasks were not mere tests of manhood, but represented achievement that filtered out to benefit the clan, tribe or race. Thus a hero was in many ways a sacrificial or disposable individual; he lived only for the good of his people.

The delights of the Goddess, therefore, are not without risk and payment. When the hero Cuchulainn failed to capture two magic birds for his wife, two dream-women, Li Ban and Fann, lashed him with whips for his failure, disabling him for a year. Clearly this theme reflects a myth in which a hero must serve the Goddess with a task, and pay a hard penalty for failure. Significantly Cuchulainn is wasted for one year, and on recovery eventually wins the love of the Otherworld women.

The motif of birds is repeated throughout Celtic mythology; in images from

Hare leaping over a tree: carving with possible religious significance from Aquae Sulis. Many Celtic myths involve totem animals and animal transformation of humans. The 'wild hunt' legend involves a Celtic god of the Otherworld hunting the spirits of the newly dead and summoning them away from the human realm. The hare may have been the totem animal of Queen Boudicca, who led a dramatic rebellion against Roman rule contemporary with the building of the Temple of Sulis Minerva: perhaps this carving commemorates her revolt and defeat.

Gaul we find goddesses with birds perched on their shoulders, and we have already discussed birds such as the owl, connected to Blodeuwedd in Welsh legend, and the raven connected to the Morrigan in Irish mythology. In Romano–Celtic images, we find Sequana, a goddess whose totem bird was the duck: she presided over the source of the river Seine, which takes its name from her.

But the motif of birds attending upon a goddess or sitting upon her shoulder, or perching upon a branch or wand which she bears, is particularly associated with those lovely but dangerous maidens of the Otherworld. Bran, son of Febhal, is charmed to the Otherworld by a maiden bearing a branch of silver with white blossoms, from the eternal apple tree of the Blessed Land; Tadhg, son of Cian, meets the divine Cliodna, the most beautiful woman in the world. She is accompanied by three magical brightly coloured birds with such sweet song that they soothe the sick and wounded to sleep; these birds feed upon the apples of the tree.

The Welsh goddess Rhiannon ('Great Queen'), associated with the horse, was also accompanied by totem birds. These sang so sweetly that they charmed the company of Bran into losing track of time:

> And there came three birds, and began singing unto them a certain song, and all the songs they had ever heard were unpleasant compared thereto; and the birds seemed to them to be at a great distance from them over the sea, yet they appeared as distinct as if they were close by, and at this repast they continued seven years.
>
> *The Mabinogion*, translated by Lady Charlotte Guest

One of the best known legends of a Maiden of Joy and Sorrow is that of Etain, made famous in literature, and the central theme of Fiona Macleod's mystical drama *The Immortal Hour*. When this allegory from Celtic tradition was set as an

83

Mastiff or lion carrying off a stag; carving with possible religious or totem animal significance from Aquae Sulis.

opera by Rutland Boughton in 1914, it touched upon the popular imagination to such an extent that it was the longest-running opera in history, and still holds the world record to this day.

Etain is an Otherworld Maiden, originally connected to the group or aspects of a horse goddess; she is of great beauty, and through a sequence of magical tribulations is parted from her true immortal realm and her divine husband Midhir. She marries the King of Ireland, Eochaidh Airemh, and forgets her origins. Eventually her immortal partner finds her, and plays chess for the right to embrace her. The significance of chess, which took at least two distinct forms in Celtic culture, was of a magical and cosmological game. The playing of board games in Celtic myth and legend always marks the interplay of great forces at work. Midhir wins his game, and returns to claim his boon. Eochaidh has the royal hall of Tara ringed by warriors; although he must keep his words and allow the kiss, the king has no intentions of allowing his beautiful wife to be carried away by Midhir. But Midhir rises through the roof of the house, and he and Etain fly away in the shape of swans.

The legend (of which the foregoing is only an extract) may be seen as an allegory of the human soul, birth and death, but it has its roots in the concept of the goddess of Sovereignty, without whom the king cannot rule.

ARIANRHOD

Arianrhod appears in Welsh Celtic mythology as one of the major characters in the *Mabinogion* story of 'Math, Son of Mathonwy'; she is the mother of Llew, who is associated with sacred kingship and Threefold Death, and of Dylan, a divine sea-child. Both children are born under mysterious circumstances, and Llew is fostered by Arianrhod's brother Gwydion, who helps him overcome three magical bindings or restrictions laid upon him by his mother, concerning his name, his bearing of arms and his marriage. In each case, these major developments of the young man's life are held in his mother's keeping. Eventually Llew gains his name and arms by subterfuge, and the flower maiden Blodeuwedd is created as his magical wife. (See Appendix for the story of Arianrhod, Llew, Blodeuwedd and the incident of the Threefold Death.)

Although the Welsh medieval extension and rationalization of the myth is confused, it still reveals the nature of Arianrhod as goddess. The legend of twin brothers born magically of a virgin, or in the case of Arianrhod one who claimed to be a virgin but was tested by magic and found to be pregnant, is repeated in various forms in Celtic mythology and folk tradition. It also has a place in world mythology, resonating through into Christianity, where the emphasis upon virginity is given a wholly different direction.

Arianrhod is ruler of Caer Sidi, a magical realm in the north; in Welsh the constellation of Corona Borealis is named Caer Arianrhod – Arianrhod's Castle. Her name means 'queen of the wheel' or 'silver wheel', and her characterization in the *Mabinogion* conceals the identity of a very powerful goddess. Some further clues as to her nature may be gained from the use of the Greek name Ariadne in the medieval Merlin texts, a name which is likely to be derived in part from a Welsh original such as Arianrhod. In the *Prophecies of Merlin* Ariadne unravels the solar system, revealing herself to be a stellar goddess of time, space and energy.

The chariot of the Moon shall disorder the Zodiac, and the Pleiades break forth into weeping. No offices of Janus shall return hereafter, but Ariadne shall lie hidden within her closed gateways. The seas shall rise up in the twinkling of an eye, and the dust of the Ancients be restored. The winds shall fight together with a dreadful blast, and their sound shall reach to the stars.

(From *The Prophecies of Merlin*, translated by J. A. Giles)

The key to the nature of this goddess is that she is a weaver, in control of the interactions of human lives and of the matter of creation itself. In Irish tradition we find that the goddess of the Land of Erin may manifest as a weaver.

Queen Medbh saw a thing that was a marvel to her, a woman standing suddenly close to her upon the shaft of her chariot, and facing her. The damsel's manner was this; in her right hand she held a weaver's sword of white bronze with seven beadings of red gold on its ends, and with this sword she wove a bordering. A spot-pied cloak of green enveloped her, and in it at her breast there was a bulging massive brooch. She had a high-coloured, rich-blooded face; a blue and laughing eye; lips red and thin; glistening pearly teeth, which indeed you might have taken for a shower of white pearls fallen and packed into her head. Like unto fresh coral were her lips. Sweeter than strings of peaked harps, played by long practised masters' hands was the sound of her voice, of her gentle utterance. Whiter than snow shed during a single night was the lustre of her skin and flesh, filtered through and past her raiment. Feet she had that were long and most white; nails pink and even, arched and pointed; fair yellow gold glittering hair; three tresses of it wound around her head, while yet another fell downwards and cast its shade below her knee.

Medbh scanned her and said, 'Girl at this time, and here, what doest thou?'

The young maiden answered, 'I reveal thy chances and thy fortunes, and Ireland's four great provinces I gather up and muster against you.'

(From 'The Cattle Raid of Cooley', *The Cuchulainn Saga*, edited by Eleanor Hull)

A curious tradition, clearly deriving from that of the classical Ariadne, yet resonating with deeper Celtic undertones, is attached to Fair Rosamund, the mistress of the English king Henry II. This legend is worth quoting in full, for it reminds us that pagan traditions were active not far beneath the surface of medieval English life:

> Henry, in the fourteenth year of his reign, caused his eldest son Henry to be crowned king of England at Westminster, giving him full power over the realm, whilst he himself was negotiated [sic] in Normandy, and his many other provinces, which after proved to his great disadvantage and trouble. In which interim, he had cast his eye upon a most beautiful lady, called Rosamund, on whom he was so greatly enamoured, that it grew even to a dotage, so that he neglected his queen's company, insomuch that she incensed all his sons, who took up arms against their father in the quarrel of their mother, by which the peace of the land was turned to hostility and uproar. Yet the king so far prevailed that he surprised the queen and kept her in close prison, and withal was so indulgent to his new mistress that he built her a rare and wondrous fabrick, so curiously devised and intricated with so many turning meanders and winding indents, that none, upon any occasion, might have access to her, unless directed by the king, or such as in that business he most trusted. And this edifice he erected at Woodstock, not far from Oxford, and made a labyrinth which was wrought like a knot in a garden, called a maze, in which any one might lose himself, unless guided by a line or thread, which, as it guided him in, so it directed him the way out.
>
> In process, it so happened, that the sons having the better of their father, set at liberty their mother, who, when the king was absent came secretly to Woodstock with her train, at such a time when the knight guarding the labyrinth was out of the way,

Wayland's Smithy, a megalithic burial mound and chamber upon the Ridgeway in Berkshire. This site was sacred to prehistoric people, who buried their ancestors or kings within it, and is likely to have had Celtic associations as a dwelling of the Underworld gods. Later Saxon associations were attached to the mound, making it the dwelling place of Wayland (from the Norse smith god Volundr). The site is close to the huge enclosed camp of Uffington Castle, and the ritual chalk carving of the White Horse (*opposite*), which probably date from the first century BC.

not dreaming of any such accident, and had left the clue of thread visibly and carelessly in the entrance. Which the queen espying, slipped not that advantage, but wound herself by that silken thread even to the very place where she found Rosamund sitting, and presenting her with a bowl of poison, she compelled her to drink it off in her presence, after which draught Rosamund within a few minutes expired. The queen departed from thence her revenge fully satisfied, for which cruel act the king could never be drawn to reconcile himself unto her afterwards . . .

Rosamund being dead, was buried in the monastery of Godstow, near unto Oxford, upon whose tomb was inscribed:

Ilic jacent in tumba, Rosamundi non Rosamund;
Non redolent, sed olet, quae redolere solet.

Which by an ancient writer was thus paraphrased into English:

The Rose of the World, but not the clean flower,
Is graven here to whom beauty was lent.
In this grave full dark now is her bower,
That in her life was sweet and redolent.
But now that she is from this life sent,
Though she were sweet, now foully doth she stink,
A mirror good for all that on her think.

Such was their English poetry in those days. Long after the death of Rosamund, there was shown in that abbey of Godstow a rare coffer or casket of hers, in which was a strange artificial motion, where were to be seen giants fighting, beasts in motion, fowls flying, and fishes swimming.

(From *The Chronographical History* of Thomas Heywood, 1641, republished 1812)

Both the Ariadne of Merlin's *Prophecies* and Fair Rosamund have faint but recognizable and significant links with Arianrhod, the Welsh goddess of the starry wheel: Ariadne reveals a cosmic or stellar power, while Rosamund, 'Rose of the World', represents the same goddess manifesting in nature, hiding at the centre of her labyrinth of delights. Just as kingship and the goddess of Sovereignty were inseparable in ancient Celtic tradition, so do we find that Arianrhod can command the naming, wedding and arming of her son Llew, who ultimately undergoes the Threefold Death of Sacred Kingship.

Likewise the much later and historical figure of Rosamund, the true love of King Henry II, is significantly revered by the common people after her death, to the extent of opposition from and final repudiation by the orthodox Church, to whom she was far too pagan a figure. She was, eventually, disinterred by the Church, to discourage the populace from praying to her as to a saint. It is worth stressing that Rosamund was a real person, to whom the mythic quality became attached; this mysterious but important process is found repeatedly in tradition.

CERRIDWEN

The Welsh crone, or goddess of dark prophetic powers, is represented by Cerridwen. Her totem animal is the sow, representing the fecundity of the Underworld, and the terrible strength of the Mother. Like many Celtic goddesses, she had two children, representing dark and light aspects emerging from the One Goddess, her daughter Crearwy being light and beautiful, and her son Afagddu being dark and ugly.

Cerridwen is keeper of the Cauldron of the Underworld, in which inspiration and divine knowledge are brewed. She brews for her son, and sets little Gwion to guard the cauldron; but three drops fall out upon his finger, and he absorbs the potency of the brew. The goddess then pursues Gwion through a cycle of changing shapes, which correspond both to totem animals and to the turning of the seasons; this theme is related to that of Mabon and Merlin, in which a divine youth is associated with the orders and creatures of Creation. The Welsh legend, however, has a significant ending, for Cerridwen, in the guise of a hen, swallows Gwion, in the guise of an ear of corn. Nine months pass, and she gives birth to a radiant child, known as Taliesin, a title attached to the greatest of Welsh poets.

Taliesin
In times past there lived in Penllyn a man of gentle lineage, named Tegid Voel, and his dwelling was in the midst of the lake Tegid, and his wife was called Caridwen. And there was born to him of his wife a son named Morvran ab Tegid, and also a daughter named Creirwy, the fairest maiden in the world was she; and they had a brother, the most ill-favoured man in the world, Avagddu. Now Caridwen his mother thought that he was not likely to be admitted among men of noble birth, by reason of his ugliness, unless he had some exalted merits or knowledge. For it was in the beginning of Arthur's time and of the Round Table.

So she resolved according to the arts of the books of the Fferyllt, to boil a cauldron of Inspiration and Science for her son, that his reception might be honourable because of his knowledge of the mysteries of the future state of the world.

Then she began to boil the cauldron, which from the beginning of its boiling might not cease to boil for a year and a day, until three blessed drops were obtained of the grace of Inspiration.

And she put Gwion Bach the son of Gwreang of Llanfair in Caereinion, in Powys, to

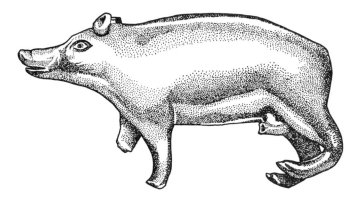

Hollow bronze boar from Ireland.

stir the cauldron, and a blind man named Morda to kindle the fire beneath it, and she charged them that they should not suffer it to cease boiling for the space of a year and a day. And she herself, according to the books of the astronomers, and in planetary hours, gathered every day of all charm-bearing herbs. And one day, towards the end of the year, as Caridwen was culling plants and making incantations, it chanced that three drops of the charmed liquor flew out of the cauldron and fell upon the finger of Gwion Bach. And by reason of their great heat he put his finger to his mouth, and the instant he put those marvel-working drops into his mouth, he foresaw everything that was to come, and perceived that his chief care must be to guard against the wiles of Caridwen, for vast was her skill. And in very great fear he fled towards his own land. And the cauldron burst in two, because all the liquor within it except the three charm-bearing drops was poisonous, so that the horses of Gwyddno Garanhir were poisoned by the water of the stream into which the liquor of the cauldron ran, and the confluence of that stream was called the Poison of the Horses of Gwyddno from that time forth.

Thereupon came in Caridwen and saw all the toil of the whole year lost. And she seized a billet of wood and struck the blind Morda on the head until one of his eyes fell out upon his cheek. And he said, 'Wrongfully hast thou disfigured me, for I am innocent. Thy loss was not because of me.' 'Thou speakest truth,' said Caridwen, 'it was Gwion Bach who robbed me.'

And she went forth after him, running. And he saw her, and changed himself into a hare and fled. But she changed herself into a greyhound and turned him. And he ran towards a river, and became a fish. And she in the form of an otter-bitch chased him under the water, until he was fain to turn himself into a bird of the air. She, as a hawk, followed him and gave him no rest in the sky. And just as she was about to stoop upon him, and he was in fear of death, he espied a heap of winnowed wheat on the floor of a barn, and he dropped among the wheat, and turned himself into one of the grains. Then she transformed herself into a high-crested black hen, and went to the wheat and scratched it with her feet, and found him out and swallowed him. And, as the story says, she bore him nine months, and when she was delivered of him, she could not find it in her heart to kill him, by reason of his beauty. So she wrapped him in a leathern bag, and cast him into the sea to the mercy of God, on the twenty-ninth day of April.

And at that time the weir of Gwyddno was on the strand between Dyvi and Aberystwyth, near to his own castle, and the value of an hundred pounds was taken in that weir every May eve. And in those days Gwyddno had an only son named Elphin, the most hapless of youths, and the most needy. And it grieved his father sore, for he thought that he was born in an evil hour. And by the advice of his council, his father had granted him the drawing of the weir that year, to see if good luck would ever befall him, and to give him something wherewith to begin the world.

The incised entrance stone at Newgrange Bronze Age Chamber, Ireland.

And the next day when Elphin went to look, there was nothing in the weir. But as he turned back he perceived the leathern bag upon a pole of the weir. Then said one of the weir-ward unto Elphin, 'Thou wast never unlucky until to-night, and now thou hast destroyed the virtues of the weir, which always yielded the value of an hundred pounds every May eve, and to-night there is nothing but this leathern skin within it.' 'How now,' said Elphin, 'there may be therein the value of an hundred pounds.' Well, they took up the leathern bag, and he who opened it saw the forehead of the boy, and said to Elphin, 'Behold a radiant brow!' 'Taliesin be he called,' said Elphin. And he lifted the boy in his arms, and lamenting his mischance, he placed him sorrowfully behind him. And he made his horse amble gently, that before had been trotting, and he carried him as softly as if he had been sitting in the easiest chair in the world. And presently the boy made a Consolation and praise to Elphin, and foretold honour to Elphin; and the Consolation was as you may see,

'Fair Elphin, cease to lament!
Let no one be dissatisfied with his own,
To despair will bring no advantage.
No man sees what supports him;
The prayer of Cynllo will not be in vain;
God will not violate his promise.
Never in Gwyddno's weir
Was there such good luck as this night.
Fair Elphin, dry thy cheeks!
Being too sad will not avail,
Although thou thinkest thou hast no gain
Too much grief will bring thee no good;
Nor doubt the miracles of the Almighty:
Although I am but little, I am highly gifted.
From seas, and from mountains,
And from the depths of rivers,
God brings wealth to the fortunate man.
Elphin of lively qualities,
Thy resolution is unmanly;
Thou must not be over sorrowful:
Better to trust in God than to forbode ill.
Weak and small as I am,
On the foaming beach of the ocean,
In the day of trouble I shall be
Of more service to thee than three hundred salmon.
Elphin of notable qualities,
Be not displeased at thy misfortune;
Although reclined thus weak in my bag,

90

There lies a virtue in my tongue.
While I continue thy protector
Thou hast not much to fear;
Remembering the names of the Trinity,
None shall be able to harm thee.'

And this was the first poem that Taliesin ever sang, being to console Elphin in his grief for that the produce of the weir was lost, and, what was worse, that all the world would consider that it was through his fault and ill-luck. And then Gwyddno Garanhir asked him what he was, whether man or spirit. Whereupon he sang this tale, and said,

'First, I have been formed a comely person,
In the court of Caridwen I have done penance;
Though little I was seen, placidly received,
I was great on the floor of the place to where I was led;
I have been a prized defence, the sweet muse the cause,
And by law without speech I have been liberated
By a smiling black old hag, when irritated
Dreadful her claim when pursued:
I have fled with vigour, I have fled as a frog,
I have fled in the semblance of a crow, scarcely finding rest;
I have fled vehemently, I have fled as a chain,
I have fled as a roe into an entangled thicket;
I have fled as a wolf cub, I have fled as a wolf in a wilderness,
I have fled as a thrush of portending language;
I have fled as a fox, used to concurrent bounds of quirks;
I have fled as a martin, which did not avail;
I have fled as a squirrel, that vainly hides,
I have fled as a stag's antler, of ruddy course,
I have fled as iron in a glowing fire,

Triple-headed figure (upon a vase) from Bavay, Nord.

I have fled as a spear-head, of woe to such as has a wish for it;
I have fled as a fierce bull bitterly fighting,
I have fled as a bristly boar seen in a ravine,
I have fled as a white grain of pure wheat,
On the skirt of a hempen sheet entangled,
That seemed of the size of a mare's foal,
That is filling like a ship on the waters;
Into a dark leathern bag I was thrown,
And on a boundless sea I was sent adrift;
Which was to me an omen of being tenderly nursed,
And the Lord God then set me at liberty.'

Then came Elphin to the house or court of Gwyddno his father, and Taliesin with him.

(From *Taliesin*, translated by Lady Charlotte Guest)

The symbols of cauldron, inspiring brew, shape changing and the rebirth of a magical or spiritual child are all under the control of the Dark Goddess; this legend is particularly fruitful when in the context of insight into the relationship between dark and light powers in Celtic religion. We might summarize Cerridwen as the goddess of transformation, for this is her ultimate role.

The shape-changing sequence was preserved in oral tradition in a number of versions, one song being collected in Somerset in the early twentieth century by the folksong collector Cecil Sharp. It seems remarkable indeed that this ancient Celtic magical chase should be remembered as a rustic entertainment by Somerset people many centuries after its pagan Celtic origins had been forgotten.

Brighid / Minerva

The goddess known as Minerva in Romano–Celtic inscriptions, or as Brighid or Saint Bride or Brigit in Celtic Christian tradition, was one of the major deities of the Celts. She represented the sister or virgin aspect of the Great Goddess, and as such her worship persisted within Roman Gaul and Britain. She also survived into the Christian era in Ireland and Scotland, where pagan–Christian prayers and ceremonies in her honour were carried out until at least as recently as the nineteenth and early twentieth centuries. She is still commemorated in folklore and Celtic tradition today as Bride or Brigit, in both Ireland and the highlands and islands of Scotland, where she was at one time regarded as the foster-mother of Jesus. We shall return to this curious Celtic belief later.

We can see a typical amalgamation of the classical Minerva with a Celtic goddess at Aquae Sulis, where dedications exist to Sul or Sulis Minerva. A fine bronze bust of the classical Minerva was found upon the site, and may be seen in the museum today. It is tempting to assume that the Roman Minerva and the Celtic Sul or Sulis were therefore identical, but this is not the case, and the example of Aquae Sulis shows how interpretation is fraught with problems. The goddess Sulis also carries dedications of her own, in which she is clearly different from Minerva, being a local variant of the chthonic or Underworld goddess (known in classical tradition as Hecate) connected to blessing, cursing and prophecy. The joint inscription, therefore, does not imply that Minerva and Sulis were identical. It is more likely that the Roman Minerva replaced another goddess, now lost to research as far as Aquae Sulis is concerned, but known as Brighid from Irish tradition, and St Brigit or Bride from Celtic and subsequently Roman Catholic Christianity.

We are reminded again of the triplicity of Celtic goddesses: a Dark Mother, a Nature Goddess or Lover, and a Sister or Virgin. The Roman Minerva, a rather stern goddess of cultural development and martial skill who is closely related to the Greek virgin goddess Athena, also owes much to a primal goddess of the Etruscans, whose culture was absorbed by the developing Romans in Italy. The Etruscan Minerva was a more warlike character, reflecting some of the savage attributes of the Irish Morrigan, goddess of battle, death and sexuality.

But the refined Minerva, who gradually merged with a native Celtic goddess (Brighid) who shared certain of her classical attributes, had lost the savage aspect to a great extent. She was patroness of cultural development, the arts and sciences, and particularly of domestic skills. In a higher form, similar to Athena,

she was patroness of certain heroes who undertook magical or spiritual tasks, mythic achievements relating to the development of humankind, but also linked directly to religious themes such as the Underworld Quest or the Sacred Kingship. We might easily see this goddess, in her Celtic form, as sister to Lugh, though this should be considered only in terms of function and not of a fixed pantheon or definite relationship. Indeed, in Romano–Celtic inscriptions,

Minerva is found paired with Mercury, who was equated with the Celtic Lugh or a similar god (see page 114).

We can discover this native Celtic goddess from Irish tradition; in *Cormac's Glossary*, written out from oral tradition in the tenth century but certainly drawing upon sources of a much earlier date, Brighid is described. She was patroness of poetry or *filidhecht*, which is the equivalent of bardic lore. The functions of *filid* and bard were to a certain extent interchangeable, the first found extensively in Ireland while the second is British; this class of poet-priest replaced the Druid order as primal retainers of culture and learning after its decimation by first Roman state then Christian opposition. As patroness of this class or order, therefore, Brighid inherited the Druidic role of a goddess of poetry, inspiration, divination.

We find that as late as the twelfth century the prophet Merlin is inspired by a feminine figure, who represents the Sovereignty of the Land of Britain, and causes his visions that reach through British history and on to the end of the solar system. In the *Vita Merlini* Minerva is made inspirer or patroness of the bard Taliesin when he describes a traditional cosmology to Merlin; this theme echoes the old union of Brighid and Minerva in Roman times. *Cormac's Glossary* also

Triple-headed statue of
Cernunnos feeding ram-
headed serpents. From
Atun, Saône-et-Loire.

states that Brighid was daughter of the Daghdha (see page 125), and had triple form. Her two sisters were patronesses of therapy and metal-work or smithing. We can see in this purely Celtic tradition, unaffected by Roman invasion, that Brighid and Minerva were, in fact, similar in many ways. They have their foundation in an ancient sister goddess of skills and inspiration, known throughout Indo-European tradition.

Brighid is further defined in Christian tradition, where she became the most popular saint of the Celts. She was worshipped in a monastery at Kildare in Ireland, where a perpetual fire was kept burning, an observance undoubtedly derived from the perpetual fires of pagan temples, suggesting that the monastery was based upon a Druidic sanctuary. The medieval historian Gerald of Wales writes that no male was allowed to enter the sacred enclosure surrounded by a hedge, in which the holy fire burned[30]. A similar perpetual fire, dedicated to Minerva by the mythical god-king Bladud, was kept burning at Aquae Sulis.

> After Hudibras came his son, Baldudus [Bladud], who reigned for twenty years and built the city of Kaerbadus, now called Bath. In it he built warm baths for the curing of diseases. He made Minerva patroness of the Baths, and in her Temple placed inexhaustible fires; these never burned down to ashes, but as soon as they began to fail, were turned into balls of stone. Baldudus was a man of great ingenuity, and taught necromancy throughout Britain, continually doing many wonderful deeds, and finally making himself wings to fly through the upper air. But he fell onto the Temple of Apollo in Ternova [Troya Nova, said to be London], his body being broken into many pieces.   (From *The History of the British Kings*, translated by Aaron Thompson)

Thus a feature of the original goddess was fire, as we would expect from a goddess of culture, inspiration and smithcraft. It is significant of Celtic perception that the fire of inspiration and the fire of the home, of poetry and of the forge are regarded as identical. There was no separation of the inner and outer worlds in our modern sense, where purely 'psychological' matters are kept separate from purely 'scientific' or physical nature. To this day in Scottish Gaelic communities Bride is remembered as patron saint of the family hearth, originally a peat fire kept burning perpetually.

In the *Life of St Brighid* we find various pagan attributes; she is associated with a magical cow, her totem animal when a pagan goddess, and she hangs her cloak upon the rays of the sun. Her dwelling place radiates light as if on fire, and her feast day is 1 February, which is to say Imbolc, the pagan spring festival. Certain Candlemass ceremonies enacted around the same time of year in Wales seem to commemorate this goddess, as they involve lighting of flames, purification with well water, and the ushering in of a new year by a fair maiden, the Queen of Heaven.

> Hail reign a fair maid with gold upon your toe,
> Open up the West Gate and let the Old year go;
> Hail reign a fair maid with gold upon your chin,
> Open up the East Gate and let the New Year in;
> Levideu sing Levideu the water and the wine,
> The seven bright gold wires and the candles that do shine.

Brigit is also known as goddess of the Brigantes, in northern England, where her

Relief carving of Minerva
or a similar goddess such as
Brighid; a head radiating
locks of hair or flames may
be seen upon her breast.

name became Brigantia, which means 'exalted one'; the Brigantes are literally the people of Brigit or Brigantia. The root word of her name means 'bright' or 'exalted', and a fundamental meaning or root word, connected with the power of fire, is also found in the title Belisima associated with Minerva. The word Bel, of course, carries a similar meaning and is associated with the god Belenos.

FOLKLORE ASSOCIATED WITH BRIDE OR BRIGIT

The continuing worship of Brigit or Bride as a Celtic (later Catholic) saint was recorded by several scholars who travelled through the highlands and islands of Scotland in the eighteenth and nineteenth centuries; some of these customs still persist today, though in a very attenuated form. We should always remember that the Celtic gods and goddesses were not abstractions or fictions; they were essential inseparable aspects of daily life. The remarkable endurance of traditions of Bride or St Brigit shows her importance very clearly, for the saint is a thinly disguised pagan goddess, unquestionably that same Brighid or Minerva known to the pre-Christian Celts in Europe, Britain and Ireland.

There are various references to Bride in Alexander Carmichael's collection *Carmina Gadelica*, which contains a vast number of Gaelic verses and prayers connected to the entire range of Celtic tradition in Scotland, as recorded in the nineteenth century. A few examples of such customs reveal the sanctity in which Bride was held by the Gaelic-speaking people.

In the Hebrides she was said to be the midwife or foster-mother of Jesus, and to have delivered him in the stable of Bethlehem, placing three drops of pure spring water upon his brow. This tale is a Christianized rationalization of an ancient Celtic myth, that of the birth of the Son of Light, and the blessing of triple purity or the three drops of wisdom upon his brow. The concept of fosterage ran through Celtic culture, and is found in a confused but important story in the Welsh *Mabinogion*, in which Pryderi is stolen away at birth but successfully fostered.

In this context of threat to a special child and fosterage, we can find connections with Christian mythology in Herod's Massacre of the Innocents, a motif also found in non-Christian myths. In Celtic tradition Bride became the foster-mother of Jesus, and is said to have worn a headdress of lighted candles to distract Herod's soldiers from the Divine Child. In the apocryphal Gospel of Thomas, a spider weaves a web to protect the infant Jesus, and this very ancient theme shows connections between the tale of the Massacre of the Innocents and the great Weaver Goddess of the ancient world.

Prayers were uttered to Bride, in the Highlands, to enable successful childbirth; we might compare this widespread tradition to the ancient Celtic custom of praying at sacred springs for successful childbirth, sometimes using votive offerings. Inscriptions of gratitude for a successful birth to goddesses of thermal springs, such as are found at Aquae Sulis, are typical of Romano–Celtic worship.

Bride was represented, on her day of 1 February (the pagan festival of Imbolc), by a doll. Young girls dressed in white processed with the image, which was usually a corn-dolly such as is found in British rural traditions even today. Gifts of food were given to the doll, and a special feast was held by the maidens, in a locked room. Eventually the youths of the community, after asking admission to pay honour to Bride, were admitted to the feast, and restraints were forgone.

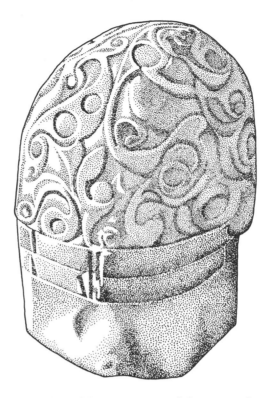

The Turoe Stone, from Co. Galway, Ireland. This appears to be an *omphalos* or navel-stone, carved with symbolic patterns. Certain stones were connected with the power and role of kingship in ancient Celtic culture.

Originally this festival of a goddess at spring and the procession of virgins would have led to a ritual mating ceremony, to bring new souls into the community. Even today certain folk ceremonies have a powerful undercurrent of sexuality and fertility.

Variants of this ceremony were found all over the Celtic world, and some seem to derive from a very primal magical worship indeed. In Ireland an image of Bride, decorated with shells and ribbons, was used to predict the forthcoming year (reminiscent of those attributes listed in the tenth-century *Glossary*, where Brighid is goddess of inspiration and prophecy). She was also associated with the totem animals cockerel and serpent, both creatures of the Underworld. Hymns were sung, and at one time there was a custom of burying a cockerel alive where three streams met on the eve of St Bride's day, or Imbolc. The hymns, in Gaelic, were of a quite pagan nature:

Early on Bride's morn
Shall the serpent come from the hole,
I will not harm the serpent,
Nor will the serpent harm me

A number of versions of this incantation, connecting 'Saint' Bride and serpents were collected in Ireland and Scotland; one included a ceremony in which an effigy of a serpent was made of peat, and beaten at the threshold of the house.

This is the day of Bride
The Queen shall come from the mound,
I will not touch the Queen
Nor will the Queen touch me

There are a number of images from pre-Christian Celtic culture of deities who clutch serpents, and the torcs which symbolize power and divinity are often serpentine. Clearly the bright and blessed Bride was originally a goddess of the Underworld, and it is in this context that we must see her amalgamation with Minerva and the chthonic goddesses in Romano–Celtic culture.

A genealogy of St Bride exists, which was chanted as a protective prayer. It links her to the ancient origins of Ireland and to the major motif of the Threefold Death, which was central to pagan Celtic religion and concepts of kingship and Sovereignty.

> The genealogy of holy maiden Bride
> Radiant flame of gold, foster-mother of Christ:
> Bride daughter of Dugal the brown
> Son of Aodh, son of Art, son of Conn,
> Son of Crear, son of Cis, son of Carmac, son of Carruin.
>
> Every day and night
> That I sing the genealogy of Bride
> Shall I not be killed, nor harried,
> Nor shall I be put in cell, nor wounded,
> Neither shall Christ leave me in forgetfulness.
>
> No fire, no sun, no moon shall burn me,
> No lake, no water, no sea, shall drown me,
> No arrow of fairy nor dart of fay shall wound me,
> And I shall be under the protection of Holy Mary
> And my gentle foster-mother my beloved Bride.

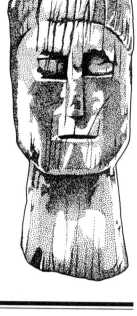

Votive head of wood, found in the river Seine. Such offerings may be designed for therapeutic invocation.

This astonishing incantation reaches back to a number of pagan religious practices and persons: Dugal the brown being the Daghdha or Good God. The averting of a death connected to the Elements echoes the theme of ritual death found in various Celtic tales. In the Welsh *Mabinogion* it is Llew who is bound by the rules of the Threefold Death, while in the Scottish, Breton and Welsh Merlin legends the motif is attached to Merlin or to a youth who is his substitute.

> There was in the hall a certain boy, one of many, and the ingenious queen, catching sight of him straightway, thought of a novel trick by which she might convict her brother [Merlin] of falsehood. So she ordered the boy to come and asked Merlin to predict what death the lad might die. Merlin answered, 'Dearest sister, he shall die, when a man, by falling from a high rock.' Smiling at these words, she ordered the boy to go away and take off the clothes he was wearing and put on others, and to cut off his long hair. She bade him come back thus that he might seem to them a different person. The boy obeyed her, for he came back to them with his clothes changed as he had been ordered to do. Soon the queen asked her brother again, 'Tell your dear sister what the death of *this* boy will be like.' Merlin answered, 'This boy when he grows up shall, while out of his mind, meet with a violent death in a tree.' . . . She then told the boy to go out and put on woman's clothing, and to come back thus dressed. Soon the boy left and did as he was bid, for he came back in woman's clothes just as though he were a woman, and he stood in front of Merlin to whom the queen said, banteringly, 'Say brother, tell me about the death of this girl.' 'Girl or not, she shall die in the river!' said her brother to her, which made King Rhydderch laugh at Merlin's reasoning, since when asked about the death of a single boy he had predicted three different kinds.
>
> For long years his prediction seemed to be an empty one, until the time when the boy grew to manhood; then it was made apparent to all and convincing to many. For while

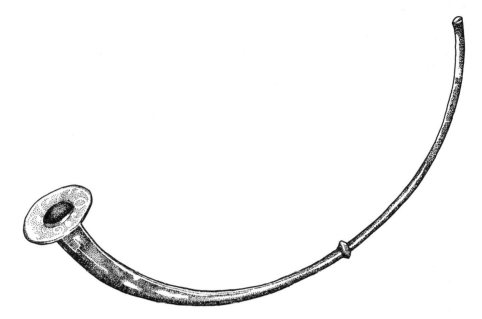

the youth was out hunting with his dogs he caught sight of a stag hiding in a grove of trees; he loosed the dogs, who, as soon as they saw the stag, climbed through unfrequented ways, and filled the air with their baying. He urged on his horse with his spurs, and followed after ... There was a high mountain surrounded on all sides by rocks with a stream flowing through the plain at its foot; thither the animal fled until he came to a river, seeking a hiding place after the usual manner of its kind. The young man pressed on and passed straight over the mountain, hunting for the stag among the rocks lying about. Meanwhile it happened, while his impetuosity was leading him on, that his horse slipped from a high rock and he fell over a precipice into the river, but so that one of his feet caught in a tree, and the rest of his body was submerged in a stream. Thus he fell, and was drowned, and hung from a tree, and by this Threefold Death made Merlin a true prophet.

(From the *Vita Merlini*, translated by J. J. Parry)

This major image is one of a number from pagan Celtic tradition, which influenced certain later developments in popular and magical imagery; the Threefold Death, as described above and in a number of other variants, is clearly shown in the Renaissance tarot card of the Hanged Man. Despite the absurd claims made for tarot in modern escapist or 'occult' literature, it certainly has clear and precise connections with sets of images found in the *Vita Merlini*, a text which predates the first known tarot cards by at least three centuries. The evidence is such that the origins of tarot seem to be rooted in story-telling traditions and images preserved by travelling entertainers, originally the bards or *filid* of Celtic culture.

In early Irish literature, drawn from an originally pagan Celtic oral tradition, a sacrificial victim is stabbed in a chamber, which is then set on fire. He runs out of the chamber to plunge his body into a vat of water (or mead) and so is drowned.

This sacrificial pattern, connected with the role of kingship, is of course repeated in the story of the Christian crucifixion, so the theme was familiar to the Celts when Christianity first arrived from the East.

The Divine Ancestor
and the Son of Light

Underpinning much of Celtic religion is the concept of ancestral descent, or ancestor worship. This should not be regarded as a crude or savage practice, for it conceals a very sophisticated psychology and metaphysics running through all legends, myths, and manifestations of the gods and goddesses, and was interwoven deeply into Celtic society. Many modern practices and beliefs from folk tradition in Celtic countries still revolve around the significance of the dead or the ancestors, and the vast subject of the Second Sight and the realms of Fairy cannot be separated from the cult of the dead. Before examining this concept further, it must be stated that it is by no means unique to the Celts.

Although Greek and later Roman religion developed along the route of an increasingly organized and formalized pantheon, classical mythology, like that of the Celts, was founded upon a cult of the dead or ancestor worship. We find many traces of it in Roman temples and households; the practice of keeping images of revered relatives in the home, the general temple dedications to *dis manibus* (the spirits of the dead), and the many myths in which heroic ancestors found or develop the tribe and nation. Ancestral lore is one of the primal and major elements of mythology and religion worldwide, though it often manifests through devious paths. We need only to consider the reverence still paid to the dead in modern Christianity to realize that the cult of ancestors has by no means vanished though it has diminished in the last fifty years.

When Julius Caesar wrote his short catalogue of Celtic gods and goddesses in Gaul, he referred to a Druidic teaching that the primal ancestor was Dis Pater, by which he meant a god similar to the Roman Dis Pater, but whose Celtic name is not recorded. *Dis* is the Underworld or realm of the dead in Roman religion, and although there was an increasing tendency to regard it as a place of shadows, it was originally a world or dimension of considerable power. The first ancestor, in primal mythology, emerged from another dimension, the Underworld, to which all his descendants return. While it gradually faded from formal or propagandist Roman Christian mythology this ancestral Underworld theme remained in Celtic myth and legend for many centuries, and persists in folk tales even today.

Although Caesar does not name the Celtic god, similar to Dis Pater, we have an Irish parallel in the figure of Donn, a dark shadowy lord who summons the dead to his island abode. As is often the case with Celtic legend, there is an actual island off the south-west coast of Ireland, known as *Tech Dunn* or the House of Donn, to which the souls of the dead are said to travel. This motif is by no means

102

Glastonbury Tor, an ancient sacred hill with many legendary attributes. In Celtic tradition it is the home of Gwyn ap Nudd, Lord of the Underworld and Master of the Wild Hunt. Like many hilltop sacred sites, the Christian dedication is to Saint Michael (the Archangel Michael), who replaced the old Celtic god of Light, known as Bel or Belenos.

unique to Ireland, for it runs through Celtic lore and has a number of examples. As a general rule the realm of the dead was either beneath the ground, or over the sea to the west; several islands off the western coasts of Wales, Ireland and Scotland have this belief attached to them. The Scilly Isles, off the extreme west of Cornwall, were known in classical times as an abode of the dead, and the striking hill of Glastonbury Tor, in Somerset, once an island in a marsh, is said to be the dwelling of Gwyn ap Nudd, a Welsh Lord of the Dead, Master of the Wild Hunt.

Donn or Dis Pater, however, is a figure behind or beyond the Lord of the Hunt, underpinning all mythology and ancestral lore. It may be significant that he is credited, in folk tradition, with control of weather, and may use it to blast or bless at will. Weather, the manifest interaction of the Four Elements, is often used as an analogy of magical and spiritual powers extending back to the original creation. We find this described very clearly in the twelfth-century *Vita Merlini*, which draws extensively upon Welsh or Breton bardic teachings, amalgamated with classical and contemporary twelfth-century knowledge[26].

Celtic tradition has a number of 'father' gods, such as the Daghdha and Nuadha, and it is clear that they do not have well-defined functions such as had developed in Roman mythology. What seems more likely is that Celtic gods and goddesses developed 'organically', in a protean manner, sharing certain traditions and attributes which were undoubtedly pre-Celtic with the complex religious lore of the Celts themselves. Thus the concept of a shadowy and all-powerful primal ancestor god is likely to be both Celtic and pre-Celtic.

We can see the figures of Donn/Dis Pater and Cernunnos as being related to one another; both are concerned with Underworld powers, both have traditions

103

regarding the souls of the dead and mastery over the energies of nature. While no clear evidence exists, it might be reasonable to suggest that gods of the Cernunnos type, of whom Gwyn ap Nudd is a variant, are the active expressions of the Lord of the Underworld, as he manifests in Nature. We might take this suggestion further and define three broad categories of god and goddess, which correspond to the Three Worlds (see Figure B, page 46):

1 Primal and chthonic (Stellar and Underworld)
2 Divine powers of creation and destruction (Solar and Planetary)
3 Forces of nature and orders of living beings (Lunar and Land).

Many of the Celtic gods and goddesses may be traced through this triple pattern, either with or without changes of identity or name as defined historically or through tradition.

THE SON OF LIGHT

The primal goddess of the Celts was the Mother, often dark and terrible, mysterious and severe. But of equal significance was her son, who we may call the Son of Light. This god, frequently identified with Apollo in classical and Romano–Celtic sources, had various forms. Not least of these was the Celtic Christ, whom we may legitimately cite as a true Celtic god. The Celts were among the first to adopt Christianity, and a Celtic Church in the West was established before the Roman Church and the advent of Roman politicial Christianity.

Indeed, early Irish records say that the Druids knew in advance of the coming of Christ, and that he was warmly accepted. While we may see this as rationalization, made by monks after the event as a type of propaganda, the early acceptance and development of a unique branch of Christianity cannot be denied. Christ was similar, if not exactly identical, to a god who had long been worshipped extensively in Celtic regions under various names: the Son of Light.

While some inscriptions and references describe the Son of Light as a type of Apollo, we should not assume that he was automatically and exclusively a solar deity . . . any more than was Apollo himself. Like all Celtic gods, he had several aspects or manifestations through the Three Worlds. The major aspects are: Bel or Belenos/Mabon/Oenghus/Christ. We may also add to this list the figure of Merlin who shares many of the attributes of the Son of Light, and may have originally been a god in his own right[31].

Perhaps the most important feature of the Son of Light is that he mediates between humanity and the supernal or infernal powers; in many cases he takes on a role similar to that of humanity, as in the case of Mabon who was imprisoned in the Underworld, or of Merlin and other characters associated with both divinity and kingship, who are sacrificed. If, as seems certain from the available evidence, this theme of a mediating and sacrificed god, the Son of Light, ran through ancient Celtic culture, then it is little wonder that Christ was absorbed into the culture so easily.

It is interesting to find that there was a Gaulish deity called Esus connected to a lost myth involving the cutting down of trees, and to totem animals of three cranes and a bull. Altars to this god were made at least three centuries before Christianity began to spread westward, and at least two hundred years before the time of Christ, so there is no possibility of borrowing or early Christian

Bracelet showing Owl Goddess, *c.* fourth century BC, Reinheim.

influence. It is just possible that the similarity of the name Jesus to that of the old god Esus may have had some significance to the pagan Celts, particularly as Jesus was a god who 'hung upon a tree' as his sacrificial act.

In this context we find a number of traditional references to trees and sacrifice, such as the ballad of 'The Two Brothers' (see page 39), which seems to echo a very primal myth of rivalry and ritual murder, a theme found in many religions of the ancient world. In 'The Leaves of Light', a powerful ballad from oral tradition that survived into the twentieth century, we find a curious merging of pagan Celtic lore and orthodox Christianity, for Jesus is found hanging 'upon a great yew tree'. The yew was traditionally the death tree, and was planted around graveyards for many centuries after its pagan origins had been virtually forgotten.

Votive figure from the source of the river Seine.

All under the leaves and the Leaves of Light
I met with Virgins Seven,
And one of them was Mary Mild,
Our Lord's first Mother in Heaven.

Oh where are you going you seven pretty maids,
All under the Leaves of Light?
Oh we are going, Thomas they said,
Seeking for a friend of thine.

And they went down into yonder town
And sat in the Gallery,
And there they saw sweet Jesus Christ
Hanging from a big Yew Tree.

Oh do not weep for me Mother,
Oh do not for me grieve.
For I must suffer this, he said,
For Adam and for Eve.

Oh how can I my weeping cease,
My sorrows to forgo,
When I must see my own Son die,
And sons I have no more?

He's laid his head on his right shoulder,
And death soon drew him nigh,
May the Holy Ghost receive my soul,
Dear Mother now I die.

Oh the rose, the gentle rose,
The fennel it grows so strong,
Amen, dear Lord, to thy Charity,
Is the ending of my song.

(Traditional carol)

The relationship between Mabon, Merlin and Christ reveals much about the nature of the Son of Light so widely worshipped by the Celts. Legends of Merlin, and reverence for him as a supernatural figure, persisted into the Middle Ages and beyond; Mabon is the central though obscure character of the Welsh *Mabinogion*, and Romano–Celtic inscriptions to him have been found in Britain. If we accept the recent theories concerning inscribed stones and structures on the eastern seaboard of the USA, then Mabon may have been worshipped more extensively than we have hitherto assumed, for an Ogham inscription to 'Mabo-Mabon' is, apparently, found at South Woodstock, Vermont, USA[32]. Better known, however, are inscriptions to Maponus from the north of England. The name Mabon simply means 'Son': he is known as Mabon, Son of Modron, or Son, Son of the Mother (Modron being a form of Matrona, the Roman name of the Great Mother Goddess).

In the *Mabinogion* and the Welsh *Triads* he is a prisoner, and one of the great heroic tasks (undertaken by Arthur and his band of warriors) is to liberate Mabon from a magical prison, which we may identify with the Underworld of Celtic mythology and religion. This theme has much in common with the youthful life of Merlin, as described by Nennius and Geoffrey of Monmouth. Merlin is a mysterious child, born of human and non-human parents; he is captured by the evil King Vortigern, and in an underground chamber is threatened with sacrifice. In response he utters prophecies, and so confounds the dark powers set against him.

The theme of poetry and prophecy dispelling darkness and creating a new world order is likely to be part of the primal myth of Mabon, a theme found in connection with Apollo (who, the Greeks claimed, was originally a Hyperborean or British god).

Both the Mabon tale in the *Mabinogion* (that of Culhwch and Olwen), and the earlier *Vita Merlini* of Geoffrey of Monmouth, involve long lists of animals extending from the earliest dawn of creation. Thus we may assume that the primal myth involved the orders of Creation and their relationship to the Son of Light.

It may be of further significance that Merlin is not only identifiable with Mabon, but also with Cernunnos. In the *Vita Merlini* he assumes the role, powers and appearance of the Horned God of the pagan Celts. Rituals involving

Romano–Celtic goddesses or nymphs from Carrowburgh, Hadrian's Wall, England.

the wearing of horns and animal costumes persisted into the present century in folk tradition, so there is no suggestion that Geoffrey of Monmouth merely fabricated this scene to entertain his readers. It may be that the youthful Mabon, in the original myth, grew up to be the great hunter Cernunnos; we have no way of knowing, though it is implied in Culhwch and Olwen that even Arthur's astonishing band of magical heroes cannot successfully hunt the savage boar Twrch Trwyth without him.

It is likely that Merlin, as a prophet, with some aspects similar to those of the shaman of Siberia, has to take upon himself certain god forms. Thus we find that Merlin has three faces or aspects: the Bright Youth, the Mad Prophet (or Lord of the Animals) and finally the Wise Elder. These are typical of three Celtic god forms, just as the Mothers are often in triple aspects:

1 Bright Youth: Mabon/Oenghus
2a Lord of Animals: Cernunnos
2b Lord of Therapy: Belenos (Apollo)
3 Wise Elder: Daghdha/Ogmios

(2a and 2b are the dark and light aspects of one another in many mythical cycles or patterns).

The themes of therapy, prophecy, healing springs, and the power of music are all associated in one phase or other with the gods listed above (though Oenghus does not seem to have a therapeutic role in Irish tradition). Significantly these themes are all associated with Merlin in Geoffrey of Monmouth's twelfth-century *Vita Merlini*, which was drawn extensively from bardic oral tradition.

We also find that in the Welsh *Triads*[19] the land of Britain is described as 'Merlin's enclosure', and that this was the first or oldest name for the island. Merlin therefore combines the various attributes of the group of gods who might be loosely equated with Apollo, and is also a type of guardian of the land. The theme of Merlin and guardianship is repeated in Arthurian legend, and in an important Welsh tradition he guards the Thirteen Treasures of Britain against a time of great need.

The name Merlin or Myrddin, when given to specific poets or seers, was likely to mean one inspired by the guardian deity of the land, and was in fact a title rather than an individual name. We find certain curious similarities between Merlin and Christ, which may hark back to the attributes of Mabon/Apollo. These include:

Virgin Birth
Persecution as a child by a corrupt king
Power of prophecy
Temptation by great powers
Ritual death.

APOLLO

To understand the generalized relationship between the Greek Apollo and the Celtic gods which share his name and are described as 'Apollo' by classical writers, we should remember the basic attributes of the Greek god. He was a god of therapy, of music, and of hunting or death. His implements were the bow and the lyre (two stringed implements representing death and life, or severity and harmony). He also was lord of the Underworld, for he conquered the great serpent Python, and took precedence in the Temple of Delphi. His son, Aesculapius, had the gift of life over death, as he had been cut alive from his dead mother's womb. Thus the superficially 'solar' god of the Greeks was typical of the ancient powers in which the sun above and below the horizon was used to represent the supernal and infernal powers, unified within one deity. Originally he would have been the Son of the Great Mother at shrines such as Delphi, but this role eventually became the less obvious one, underpinning the overt status of the god and the shrines with a chthonic esoteric tradition that tapped into ancient cultural origins and magical forces.

Double-headed stone figure, possibly of the Cernunnos type, from Hölzgerlingen, Württemburg.

Apollo has many dedications in Celtic regions under Roman control: but we should always bear in mind that these do not necessarily imply the classical Greek god Apollo, but are approximations or equivalents based upon a Celtic god with similar attributes. As Celtic gods also had numerous localized individual manifestations and names, we will find that there were many variants upon Apollo in Celtic worship. Caesar describes the Gaulish Apollo as a therapeutic deity, driving away disease. Celtic gods of the Apollo group are certainly associated with thermal springs, and at Aquae Sulis (Bath, England) a flaming head was carved with distinctly solar attributes. Tradition also associates with Bath the figure of king Bladud, a flying man who embodies a myth of regeneration, implying many regal solar attributes.

The god-name Belenos is directly linked to Apollo in Romano–Celtic inscription; he was the god of the Celtic kingdom of Noricum in the eastern Alps, but was also known in Britain and Ireland, as well as Italy and southern Gaul. The word *bel* means 'bright' or 'brilliant', and is found in various place-names which may derive from the cult of this Celtic Apollo. The Irish ceremony of Beltane, known as May Day in Britain, marked the beginning of the Celtic summer. Ceremonies of regeneration, purification with spring water and fire-lighting are still connected to this day with Beltane.

In the Romano–British temple of Sulis Minerva (Bath), there is firm evidence of the worship of Apollo and Aesculapius, each part of the Greek Apollonian cult adopted by the Romans. As this temple is over copious thermal springs, we may assume that the Celtic god of the site was of the Belenus type. Indeed, the traditional name of King Bladud might be compounded from the Celtic language elements of Bel and dud, meaning bright and dark[33]. Among the various inscriptions associated with Belenos and the Apollo group of gods are the following:

Atepomaros: 'possessing great horses', perhaps connecting a native deity to the theme of Apollo and his chariot and horses which ride through the sky bearing the light of the sun.

Grannus: this name may be associated with the Irish Grian or Grianainech, a title for the god Oghma, meaning 'Sun-face'. Grannus was invoked by the Emperor Caracalla in AD 215 in association with Aesculapius and Serapis, both gods of the cult of the Therapeutae. Grannus is often found in association with Sirona, a goddess whose name means 'star'. This connection is reminiscent of the concept of Three Worlds (Star, Sun and Moon) which underpins Celtic mythology (see Figure B, page 46).

A cosmology or pattern of worlds, leading from the Underworld to the Stars, is clearly shown on the temple pediment of Aquae Sulis, with the solar god as the major figure in its centre, with wings, flaming hair, staring eyes, prominent ears (all-hearing) and a huge serpent-headed neck torc, symbol of divinity and power.

In Gaul the god-name Bormo or Borvo is associated with seething or boiling waters, and he is another variant of the Apollo type. He is paired with the goddess Damona, or 'Divine Cow'. The cow as totem animal is also associated with the Celtic goddess/saint Bride or Brigit, as a creature of nourishment, and further associated with a magical tub or cauldron of plenty. The cauldron symbolism would have been associated with thermal springs as they were clear evidence of the seething boiling energies of the Underworld.

MABON OR MAPONUS

As we have mentioned previously, this Divine Youth appears as a hero in the Welsh legends of the *Mabinogion*, where King Arthur's heroes need his assistance to hunt a giant boar, the Twrch Trwyth. The story, drawn from a medieval Welsh manuscript collection but undoubtedly deriving from a much earlier oral story-telling tradition of the Celtic bards, is supported by archaeological evidence. Maponus was worshipped in the north of Britain and in Gaul, and is further associated with therapeutic springs. In Welsh tradition he is Mabon son of Modron (son of the Mother), held captive since he was stolen from his mother at the age of three days. He is equated in a Romano–Celtic inscription with Apollo Citharoedus, 'the player of the lyre'. Thus he was a youthful god of the Apollo type, connected to therapy, music and a ritual hunt. Furthermore his legend suggests that he is linked to the orders of creation, for an increasingly complex and elder cycle of animals lead the Arthurian warrior to rescue him.

Arthur said 'which marvel shall we seek first?' 'It will be best,' said they, 'to seek Mabon the son of Modron . . .'. They went forward until they came to the Ousel of Cilgwri. And Gwrhyr adjured her for the sake of Heaven, saying, 'Tell me if thou knowest aught of Mabon the Son of Modron, who was taken when three nights old from between his mother and the wall.' And the Ousel answered, 'When first I came here, there was a smith's anvil in this place, and I was then a young bird. And from that time no work has been done upon the anvil, save the pecking of my beak every evening, and now there is not so much as the size of a nut remaining thereof; yet the vengeance of Heaven be upon me, if during all that time I have ever heard of the man for whom you inquire. Nevertheless I will do that which is right, and that which is fitting that I should do for an embassy from Arthur. There is a race of animals who were formed before me, and I will be your guide to them.' So they proceeded to the place where was the Stag of Redynvre. 'Stag of Redynvre, behold, we are come to thee, an embassy from Arthur, for we have not heard of an animal older than thou. Say, knowest thou aught of Mabon, Son of Modron, who was taken from his mother when three nights old?' The Stag said, 'When first I came hither, there was a plain all around me, without any trees save one oak sapling, which grew up to be an oak with a hundred branches. And that oak has since perished, so that now nothing remains of it but the withered stump; and from that day to this I have been here, yet I have never heard of the man for whom you inquire. Nevertheless, being an embassy from Arthur, I will be your guide to a place where there is an animal which was formed before I was.'

So they proceeded to the place where was the Owl of Cwm. 'Owl of Cwm Cawlwyd, here is an embassy from Arthur; knowest thou aught of Mabon, Son of Modron, who was taken after three nights from his mother?' 'If I knew I would tell you. When first I came hither, the wide valley you see was a wooded glen. And a race of men came and rooted it up. And there grew a second wood, and this wood I am in is the third. My wings, are they not withered stumps? Yet all this time, even until today, I have never heard of the man for whom you inquire. Nevertheless, I will be the guide of Arthur's embassy until you come to the place where is the oldest animal in this world, and the one that has travelled the most, the Eagle of Gwern Abwy.'

Gwrhyr said, 'Eagle of Gwern Abwy, we have come to thee, an embassy from Arthur, to ask thee if thou knowest aught of Mabon the Son of Modron, who was taken from his mother when he was three nights old.' The Eagle said, 'I have been here for a great space of time, and when I first came hither there was a rock here, from the top of it I pecked at the stars every evening; and now that rock is not so much as a span high. From that day to this I have been here, and I have never heard of the man for whom you enquire, except once when I went in search of food as far as Llyn Llyw. And when I came there I struck my talons into a salmon, thinking that he would serve me as food for a long time. But he drew me into the deep, and I was scarcely able to escape from him . . . unless he knows something of him whom you seek, I cannot tell who may. However, I will guide you to the place where he is.'

So they went thither, and the Eagle said, 'Salmon of Llyn Llyw, I have come to thee with an embassy from Arthur, to ask thee if thou knowest aught concerning Mabon, Son of Modron, who was taken away at three nights old from his mother.' 'As much as I know, I will tell thee,' replied the Salmon. 'With every tide I go upward along the river, until I come near to the walls of Gloucester, and there I have found such wrong as I never found elsewhere. And that you may give credence thereto, let one of you ride thither upon each of my two shoulders.'

So Kai and Gwrhyr Gwalstawd Ieitheodd went upon the two shoulders of the Salmon, and they proceeded until they came to the wall of the prison, and they heard a great wailing and lamenting from the dungeon. Said Gwrhyr, 'Who is it that laments in this house of stone?' . . . 'It is Mabon the Son of Modron who is here imprisoned, and no imprisonment was ever so grievous as mine . . .'

(From 'Kilhwch and Olwen', *The Mabinogion*, translated by Lady Charlotte Guest)

OENGHUS

The Irish equivalent of Maponus is Oenghus Mac in Og, 'the Young Lad'. He is son of the Daghdha, the greatest Irish god, born of a secret union with Boann, the river goddess. He is said to dwell in the prehistoric mound of the Bruigh na Boinne, which he tricked away from his father. Although Oenghus is a bright young god, born of primal powers, he is not associated with therapeutic springs. Oenghus is a figure of great beauty, wit and charm, and is also associated with fatal love in Irish legends. The Scottish poet William Sharp (writing as 'Fiona Macleod' in the nineteenth century with a profound knowledge of Celtic mythology and language) rightly described Oenghus as 'Lord of Love and Death'. In this last context we may see once again a link with the primal Apollo, whose bolt could bless or blast.

CERNUNNOS

We now come to one of the most maligned of the pagan Celtic gods . . . one who is misrepresented not only by his cult opponents, but by those who claim to be his modern-day revivalist supporters. He is Cernunnos, the Horned One, a god

Carving of serpent coiled around a tree, usually associated with Aesculapius, the god of the Theraputae. Tree and serpent symbolism was also central to Celtic religion (from Aquae Sulis).

of such importance to the Celts that the early Christian Church made him a special target of abuse, using his image in a warped manner as that of the Devil, *deo falsus*, or false god. In modern paganism many attempts have been made to revive and justify worship of the Horned One, ranging from extremes of self-gratification and sexual licence to serious research into his Celtic and pre-Celtic origins; regrettably the second class of revival enthusiasts is far smaller than the first.

It should be stated emphatically that this deity has far less to do with 'fertility' and sexuality than is assumed in popular fantasy, for he is a god of hunting, culling and taking. His purpose is to purify through selection or sacrifice, in order that powers of growth and fertility may progress without stagnation. In this context of purification and de-pollution, he should be an especially interesting figure to us today, for he represents certain truths known to our ancestors which have been neglected by us at our peril.

Horned gods are known from very early imagery, dating back to prehistoric times. We have the figure of Cernunnos from a variety of Celtic sources, the earliest being from Val Camonica in northern Italy. In this simple image, dating from around the fourth century BC, we find symbolic attributes that are also known from Romano–Celtic sources: the horns, serpents and the torc. The name of Cernunnos is found on a relief from Paris (found close to the enigmatic relief of Esus), and this is the sole source for the name in relief inscription. But we do find that the name and image of Cernunnos are preserved in a number of British sources and legends, for there are a variety of place names bearing the word Cerne, and the enduring legend of Herne the Hunter, an antlered woodland being, dwelling in Windsor Forest.

Although the Val Camonica relief shows a standing figure apparently wrapped in a long robe, the majority of images of the Horned One show him seated in a characteristic cross-legged position. This posture has frequently caused writers to speculate upon Eastern origins for the god, and is inaccurately called the 'Buddhic' posture. Such comparisons are extremely misleading; the cross-legged posture is that of a hunter at rest, typical of those squatting or cross-legged positions adopted by hunters worldwide, and commonplace among people who live mainly in the open. Furthermore, we have reports from classical writers that the Gauls sat not upon couches or stools, but upon the ground. Thus the cross-legged posture of Cernunnos and other deities reveals his function, and does not imply that he has an Eastern origin any more than cross-legged or lotus-position images in the East imply a Celtic or American Indian origin.

The most dramatic representation of Cernunnos is that upon the Gündestrup Cauldron (see illustration on page 29), where he holds a ram-headed serpent in his left hand, and sits cross-legged. To his right stands a stag, bearing antlers similar to those of the god himself, and other animals are in attendance. The serpent is the totem creature of fire from within the earth, and ram-headed serpents held a special significance to the Celts as emblems of power. Romano–Celtic images of the Horned One sometimes show him with a sack of coins, which he pours forth upon the ground. This is likely to be a later development of his connection with the Underworld powers of increase, and we have seen it attached to other Celtic deities such as the Celtic 'Mercury'.

Serpent imagery is found in Celtic tradition connected with the Ulster hero Connall Cernach, and with the Gaelic St Brigit or Bride; both are found in legends involving the taming of serpents. In the case of Brigit, a ritual prayer or ceremony was preserved in tradition concerning serpents, and was reported as late as the nineteenth century. Such themes are reminiscent of images from the

Romano–Celtic period, in which the Horned One holds a serpent, or feeds serpents coiled around his waist.

We find the lordship of animals and the wearing of horns in Welsh tradition, for in the *Mabinogion* a giant herdsman is found, to whom all the animals bow as to a lord (see page 59).

In the twelfth-century *Vita Merlini* Merlin takes on the role of Lord of the Animals and, wearing stag's horns, summons a vast herd of stags and she-goats. It is interesting to find that in this legend Merlin is married to Guendoloena, a type of flower maiden. It suggests, along with other legendary evidence, that the Lord of the Animals and the Lady of Nature or of Flowers were originally a pair, just as we find certain of the other Celtic gods and goddesses paired[34].

> So he went about all the woods and groves and collected a herd of stags in a single line, and the deer and she-goats likewise, and he himself mounted a stag. And when day dawned he came quickly, driving the line before him to the place where Guendoloena was to be married. When he arrived Merlin forced the stags to stand patiently outside the gates while he cried aloud, 'Guendoloena! Guendoloena! Come! Your gifts are awaiting you!' Guendoloena came quickly, smiling and marvelling that the man was riding upon a stag and that it obeyed him, and that he could get together so large a number of animals and drive them before him just as a shepherd does the sheep that he is in the habit of driving to the pastures.   (From the *Vita Merlini*, translated by J. J. Parry)

The Horned One was not easily supplanted, therefore, by orthodox Christianity, and his image remained active not only in legend but in folk ritual. St Augustine forbade 'that most filthy habit of dressing up as a horse or stag' in the fourth century AD, yet it was preserved in many folk dances and rituals well into the present era.

CERNUNNOS AND THE DEVIL

As mentioned briefly above, the Horned God became an especial target of the early Church. The Christian Devil is a fusion of the old Celtic Cernunnos or Lord of the Animals, the classical god Pan who shared certain functions with Cernunnos, and the Middle Eastern *shaitan* or adversary. As often happens when images from quite different cultures are artificially merged through dogma supported by force of arms, the result was something suppressive and unhealthy.

We can see this process in the development of tarot images, which were formalized during the Renaissance from ancient oral story-telling repertoires of travelling poets. The Tarot Trumps are found in the much earlier *Vita Merlini*, pre-dating the first known tarot cards by about three centuries and including clear descriptions of images such as the Empress, the Hanged Man, the Wheel of Fortune, the Fool and so on. But these earliest 'tarot' images are derived from bardic tradition preserving Celtic traditions of gods, goddesses and cosmology: the orthodox trumps of Death as a skeleton and the Devil do not appear. In their stead we have the Celtic Death Goddess (also found in the *Prophecies of Merlin*) and the Lord of the Animals (a phase or image taken on by Merlin himself). Although such images were changed radically by the political Church, they did not pass from the common imagination. (For a full examination of the development of tarot, see *The Merlin Tarot* by R. J. Stewart and Miranda Gray, published by Aquarian Press in 1988.)

The Celtic Gods

LUGH, OR MERCURY

It seems likely that one of the most widespread gods in the Celtic realms at the time of the Roman conquest was similar to the classical Mercury. There are more statues and inscriptions to him than to any other Celtic deity, though we should be cautious in assuming that this automatically means that he was the greatest god. He certainly played an important part in the lives of the Celts, being patron of (according to Caesar) all the arts, travelling and influence in money and commerce. When Caesar refers to arts, he means skills or abilities rather than arts in the modern sense, though the term did include artistic skills. The Celts had artistic skills of the highest standard, as their metalwork, jewellery and varied complex carvings clearly show.

The Celtic Mercury, a god of many skills, or perhaps the god of the essence and distribution of skill (hence his patronage of so many areas of daily life that require ability, such as travel, commerce, artistic or craft skills), was also a god of war. Clearly he was not identical to the classical Mars, but war was included as an artistic skill by the Celts: we can see this in the Cuchulainn saga, where the warrior's ability and his weapons and costume are described in high poetry.

To fight Cuchulainn, the Hound of Ulster, was no small task. When the great and terrible hero Ferdiad made himself ready for battle, he put on his magical armour before the coming of Cuchulainn.

First came a kilt of striped silk, with a border of spangled gold next to his white skin. Outside, well sown over it, was an apron of brown leather to protect the lower part of his body. And over that again he placed a stone, which was as big as a millstone for his protection. And on top of all this, he put on his firm deep apron, made of purified iron. He wore this on top of the great stone, and all through dread of GAE BOLGA, the terrible spear of Cuchulainn.

Upon his head he wore a crested battle helmet, on which were four gems flashing in each quarter, at the East, at the South, at the West, and at the North. This battle helmet was studded all over, with crystals and precious stones and with the brilliant rubies of the eastern world.

In his right hand, he took his destructive sharp-pointed strong spear. On his left side hung his curved battle sword, with a golden hilt and red pommel of pure gold. He slung upon his back a huge shield, upon which were fifty rounded shield-bosses. Each of these bosses would bear the weight of a full grown hog, while in the very centre of the shield was a great central boss of red gold.

(From *The Cuchulainn Saga*, edited by Eleanor Hull)

Battle was often a ritual art rather than a bloody slaughter, though the Celts eventually adopted (to a limited extent) a Roman style of warfare when it became clear that the invaders would not settle for ritual combat, heroic contests or judgements by Druids in place of actual battle to the end between opposing forces.

The Romano—Celtic images of the Celtic Mercury often show a young handsome man, with the symbols of caduceus and purse. His totem animals were the ram, cock and tortoise. While these attributes are typical of the Greek god and his Roman variants, we also find Mercury shown as a bearded and more mature god, possibly the older Celtic form. He is frequently partnered by a goddess called Rosmerta or Maia who represents the abundance of wealth or material benefit; the symbolism is clear: skill and ability are joined to the natural abundance of the earth or land in a literal sense in terms of metal-working, travel or other artistic endeavours.

We are, to a certain extent, forced to call this god of skill 'Mercury', as his Celtic name from Gaul is not known. He was so widespread that the Celts themselves had no trouble in combining his older form with the youthful classical god of Greece and Rome who had similar attributes. But in Ireland, where the Romans did not invade, the god Lugh is the equivalent of the Gaulish Mercury. He was known as *sam ildanach*, 'skilled in many arts simultaneously', and many tales are recounted of his abilities. He was, therefore, the god of ability or skill.

Lugh was also known in other Celtic lands, and his name remains in place names in Britain and Europe, such as Lyons (France), Leiden (Holland) and even Carlisle in northern England. These and other place names are derived from the name Lugodunum, the town or enclosure of Lugh. Some writers have suggested

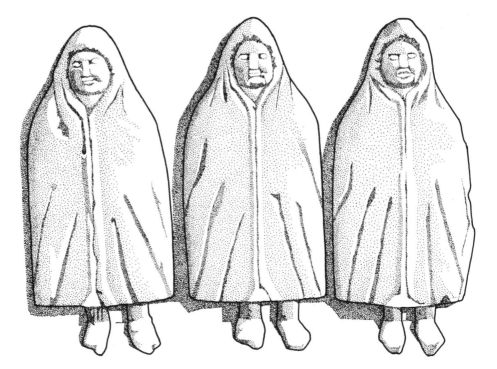

Hooded gods from Housesteads, Northumberland, England. These mysterious figures always appear in triple form.

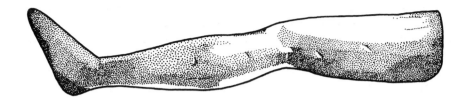

that London is also derived from Lugodunum, though this seems less likely.

The god Lugh, master of all skills equally, is still celebrated today by the Irish Celts, as he has been for many thousands of years, on 1 August. This festival was originally called Lughnasadh, the day of Lugh. In time this festival became Lammas, the harvest festival associated with the first ripening of the corn. The ceremonies of Lammas originally included sports and games of skill, and the persistence of the harvest festival as a semi-Christian rite, in which the first loaves were consecrated in churches, reveals how important it was in the lives of the Celts. Lugh was associated with the first harvest as consort of the goddess of abundance.

The Irish tale of the Battle of Magh Tuiredh demonstrates clearly how Lugh was seen by the Celts. He was at first refused admission to the royal hall of Tara, for he claimed in turn to be skilled in abilities that were already well represented within: wheelwright, metal-worker, warrior, bard, magician, doctor, cupbearer and more. But only Lugh combined all these skills within one person, and thus was permitted to enter. He is also said to have invented certain typically Celtic skills and games, such as ball games, horsemanship and *fidchell* (the symbolic board game of the Irish Celts, often called 'chess' in translations). It is interesting to note that these three 'games' all have a magical cosmological and ritual significance in cultures worldwide, and were certainly regarded as religious and magical activities by the Celts.

The myth of Lugh, which would have been of central importance to the Celts in its various forms, thus includes the prevalence of many skills, and the wedding of these skills to the potential or unrealized abundance of the land. After his admission to Tara, the royal centre of the land of Ireland, Lugh eventually deputizes or acts as steward for King Nuadha, who had lost his hand in battle (until it was replaced by a silver hand, thus gaining Nuadha the title Argetlam or 'Silver-Hand'). This is an important theme, though often confused by the passage of time. Originally it may have meant that Lugh/Mercury, god of all skills, was the spirit that inspired the king or hero. Celtic kings were literally wedded to the land, which was represented by various goddesses, all of whom were collected under the general figure now known as 'Sovereignty'.

While Lugh was steward for the wounded Nuadha (no maimed king could remain upon the royal throne) and eventually came to rule after Nuadha's death, he was also patron or spiritual father of Cuchulainn, the great Irish hero. When King Conn of the Hundred Battles, one of the greatest Irish kings of Tara, had a vision of Lugh, he found him enthroned with the goddess of Sovereignty of Ireland. This is perhaps equivalent to the Gaulish dedications and partnership of Mercury and Rosmerta mentioned above.

In Welsh legend we find Llew described in the *Mabinogion* tale of Math and Mathonwy; he is eventually married to a maiden of flowers called Blodeuwedd. Curiously Llew is shown as being skilled in shoe-making (among other skills that he is forced to adopt in exile), and an inscription still survives today at Osma in Spain from the Guild of Shoemakers, who dedicated a statue to the Lugoves in Romano–Celtic times. The pluralizing of the god's name is typical of Celtic religion, where gods and goddesses were frequently represented in triple form. The motif of gaining skills through adversity, and against opposition, which is a feature of the story of Llew, is a typical magical or educational allegory of growth and development.

Lugh's name means 'light' or 'shining', and he is represented in Irish legends as being the triumph of light over darkness. He was guardian or rightful user of the magical spear of Gorias, and was particularly associated with the use of the slingshot, with which he killed the terrible adversary Balar. Thus we can see in him attributes not only of Mercury and Mars, but also of certain aspects of Apollo. As usual when dealing with Celtic gods, we must never use the classical near-equivalents as 'authorities' or 'originals'; their predominance is merely an accident of history and literature, and should never be employed as magical, spiritual or religious dogma. Lugh is often described as Lugh Lamhfhada in Irish tradition . . . Lugh of the Long Arm. His magical sling and spear are not merely suggestive of killing at a distance (long arm), but are typical attributes of power in a god of victory and light.

We can see the theme of Lugh recurring in medieval Arthurian legends, which emerged from Celtic culture after the collapse of Rome, but were based upon a much earlier stratum of tales and legends preserved by bards. Lancelot is similar in many ways to Lugh . . . his many skills, his apparent role as replacement for the wounded or impotent King Arthur, and his rivalry for Guenevere, who is partially derived from the old Celtic nature or flower goddess[35]. The relationship between Arthur, Guenevere, Lancelot and the well-being of the land and people is a restatement of the pagan Celtic theme of Sovereignty. Thus the triadic pattern of the three major Arthurian characters deals, like the obscure *Prophecies of Merlin*, with the Sovereignty of Britain[1].

NUADHA OF THE SILVER ARM

As king of the Tuatha De Danann, Nuadha was first deprived of kingship due to the loss of his hand in battle, then gave kingship over to the multi-skilled Lugh who was better able to handle the war with the terrible Fomhoire. We find this pattern echoed, albeit in a faint manner, in the legend of King Arthur and Lancelot in later British and European sources, for a wounded king may not rule and must be replaced by a successor. In medieval Scotland the elected kings, installed in the ancient Celtic manner, chose a *tanist* or successor; this custom seems to hark back to an ancient myth in which two brothers, light and dark, compete for the love of the Goddess of the Land. It was typical of the Celts that they enacted culturally and socially the deepest themes of their religion and mythology[36].

In the *Mabinogion* tale of Culhwch and Olwen a hero called Lludd Llaw Ereint appears, who seems to be derived from the Welsh equivalent of Lludd or Nudd of the Silver Hand. We find that Lludd is of great mythical importance in the Welsh legend of Ludd and Llevelys in which two dragons battle for supremacy, but are finally trapped in the centre of the land and kept imprisoned in a container underground. This symbol of the fighting dragons is central to the

Merlin cosmology found in the *Prophecies* and *Life of Merlin*, and may have been a major emblem for Druidic instruction concerning cosmology, polarity of powers and prophecy.

Both the Irish Nuadha and the Welsh Lludd are concerned with themes in which the king gives up his kingship or consults a brother to rid the land of plague; both tales deal with the essential foundation of sacred kingship and the sovereignty or protection of the land. The images of waste land, redemptive quest and brotherly rivalry for a queen are of course highly developed in the Arthurian and Grail literature. We may safely assume that the entire Arthurian and Grail corpus derives from an early pagan motif concerned with kingship, sovereignty and regeneration[37].

There is further evidence for Nuadha or Nudd from Romano–Celtic Britain, for a large temple complex at Lydney on Severn is dedicated to the god Nodons; and the name is found in other parts of Britain also, associated with Mars but in a therapeutic role rather than warlike. The god Nodons was connected to water and to healing, and his totem animal seems to have been the dog. The presence of a votive bronze arm in the Lydney Park temple is suggestive of the silver arm of Nuadha, but may equally be a votive offering pleading for healing of an affliction. The evidence from Ireland, Wales and other parts of Britain suggest that Nudd or Nuadha was a major deity of the Celts, concerned with kingship, therapy and the power of water.

THE SMITH GOD

Julius Caesar does not list Vulcan (the classical smith god) in his description of the Celtic gods of Gaul, yet smithcraft was highly regarded by the Celts, and a smith god is certainly known from various sources. The triple goddess Brighid, for example, was patroness of inspiration, therapy and smithing, and the craft of the smith or metal worker was developed to a high degree by the Celts. Romano–Celtic carvings of a smith god, sometimes bearing tongs and hammer, are known in Britain; he is also associated with Mars, or with Celtic gods similar to Mars such as Toutates.

The smith was always associated with magical powers, for he, or she in the case of Brighid, mastered the primal element of fire and moulded the metals of the Underworld through skill and strength. This magic of the smith is often said, quite incorrectly, to be a superstition developed out of the change-over from stone to bronze and bronze to iron in early cultures, as if technology alone was a mystery; such an explanation is insufficient, for there is a close connection between concepts of smithcraft and concepts of the creation of the world, in which the Elements of Air, Fire, Water and Earth are fused together in a new shape. Smiths are frequently associated with supernatural powers, including therapy, in folklore, so it is no surprise that the ancient smith gods were credited with similar magical abilities.

In Irish mythology the divine smith is known as Goibhniu, and he is accompanied by two further aspects, or brothers or associates in typical Celtic triple form: Creidhne, god of metal-working, and Luchtaine, divine wheelwright. We can see the significance of this triad when we consider that the pagan Irish culture was, in one sense, an aristocratic heroic warrior society: such crafts were fundamental to survival and development. But we should also remember that warrior skills and 'aristocracy', which is perhaps an unfortunate modern

Celtic Christian cross base, from the island of Iona, Scotland.

term to employ, were part of a fundamentally matriarchal society, as is clearly shown by the role of goddesses and queens in Celtic myth, history and legend.

We find the three craft gods making weapons and carrying out repairs for the divine Lugh and the entire Tuatha De Danann at the battle of Magh Tuiredh where the powers of light fought the powers of darkness: the resulting objects were magically empowered. This heroic tradition may be seen initially as an ideal myth for a warrior culture, but it runs far deeper than the surface theme, for it is an analogy of the creation of the world or worlds.

Smith gods are associated with the important theme of the Otherworld Feast, which is found in Celtic, Greek and Indian mythology, and has many other parallels worldwide. Goibhniu was host at a feast in which his guests were rendered immortal through a magical, intoxicating drink. Similar themes are found in Indian tradition, while the Greek smith god Hephaestos serves the gods with drink. In Welsh tradition the god is known as Gofannon (both the Irish and Welsh names derive from a root word for 'smith'), and an old Welsh law ruled that in a chieftain's court the smith should have the first drink of any feast.

The theme of the regenerative Otherworld or Underworld was of great importance to the Celts, and ultimately led to the medieval heretical pagan—Christian legends of the Holy Grail. The Grail derives from an Underworld cauldron of immortality; such a cauldron once belonged to the Daghdha, and another was given as a gift by the god-king Bran in the story of Branwen in the Welsh *Mabinogion*.

'And I will enhance my gift,' said Bendigeid Vran 'for I will give unto thee a cauldron, the property of which is, that if one of the men be slain today, and be cast therein, tomorrow he will be as well as ever he was at his best, except that he will not regain his speech.'
(From 'Branwen the Daughter of Llyr', *The Mabinogion*, translated by Lady Charlotte Guest)

On the Gündestrup cauldron one of the images shows a line of warriors assembling in front of a huge vat or cauldron, into which a giant figure or god plunges them one by one to be renewed and ride away. There is a connection between this theme and imagery and the use of a cauldron or vat of intoxicating drink as one of the elements of the kingly Threefold Death, though it is unwise to draw exact comparisons. (See Appendix for the story of 'Math Son of Mathonwy', and page 100 for the Threefold Death in the *Vita Merlini*.)

In later Irish tradition the divine smith becomes a great builder, or a resourceful master mason. Similar traditions are preserved in England in the figure of Wayland Smith, who owes much to both Celtic and Saxon origins; he too is a giant smith who forged wonders and presided over the ancient road of the Ridgeway, where he is associated with a prehistoric burial mound, Wayland's Smithy (see page 86). This site is close to the great earthworks of the Belgae at the White Horse, Uffington, and was a potent place of ancestral magic millennia before the Saxons came to England.

Wayland's Smithy is an excellent example of the manner in which successive culture, divinities and myths are merged, in time, through the agency of the land itself. The Smith remains today as a legendary figure, having passed from a prehistoric role as a sacred ancestor within a burial mound, to the skill and craft of a Celtic god, to the Saxon and Norse Volundr, a smith god or hero of mighty deeds and power. The resulting fusion creates a distinctive yet harmonious British god, representing many phases of history and magic or religion, deeply rooted in the land, and specifically located in one region. These are abiding requirements of magical images attuned to a sacred landscape[38].

The land is itself a sovereign power, simultaneously an agency of transformation and preservation through time. When we encounter such profound but slow organic transformations and harmonizations of varied influences, we should be reminded of the story of Arthur and Morgen, the Otherworld priestess, mistress of the Fortunate Island. She examined the wounded king and said that she could heal him, in time, if he remained with her.

> The Island of Apples which men call 'The Fortunate Isle' gets its name from the fact that it produces all things of itself; the fields there have no need of the ploughs of the farmer, and all cultivation is lacking except that which nature provides. Of its own accord it produces grain and grapes, and apple trees grow in its woods from the close-clipped grass. The ground of its own accord produces everything over and above mere grass, and people live there a hundred years or more.
>
> Nine Sisters rule there by a pleasing set of laws those who come to them from our own country. She who is first of them is most skilled in the healing art, and excels her sisters in the beauty of her person. *Morgen* is her name, and she has learned what useful properties all the herbs contain, so that she can cure sick bodies. She also knows an art by which to change her shape, and to cleave the air on new wings like Daedalus; when she wishes she can be at Brest, Chartres or Pavia, and when she wills, she slips down from the air on to your shores . . .
>
> There after the battle of Camlann we took the wounded Arthur, guided by *Barinthus* to whom the waters and the stars of heaven were well known. With him steering the ship we arrived there with the king, Morgen receiving us with fitting honour, and in her chamber she placed the king upon a golden bed, and with her own hand she uncovered his honourable wound and gazed at it for a long time.
>
> At length she said that health could be restored to him if he stayed with her for a long time and made use of her healing art. Rejoicing, therefore, we entrusted the king to her, and returning spread our sails to the favouring winds.
>
> (From the *Vita Merlini*, translated by J. J. Parry)

GODS OF THE SEA

The Celts were nothing if not adaptable and variable; in some areas they became great sea-faring people. During the first century AD Julius Caesar described the powerful ocean-going ships of the Veneti, a tribe living in the region of present day Brittany (see page 30).

Although the Romans destroyed the sea-going might of the Celts in Europe, more by luck than skill as Caesar himself admitted, the sea-girt lands of Britain and Ireland still produced merchants, fishermen and sea-going travellers in abundance.

In Irish tradition the best-documented sea god is Manannan mac Lir, whose name means, simply, Manannan Son of the Sea. The Isle of Man, situated between Ireland and Britain in the Irish Sea, is associated with this god, who may be relatively local to that area. He is not, for example, an overall ocean god, and though we find that Nodons was occasionally equated with Neptune in Roman Celtic Britain, no such equation is known for Manannan. In Britain, however, in later Celtic tradition, the name Manawydan ap Llyr appears, though not as a sea god.

Although clearly a god, Manannan mac Lir is not associated with the Tuatha

120

De Danann, and does not fight in the two great battles of Mag Tuiredh. Another sea god, Tethra, does fight with the Fomhoire against the Tuatha De Danaan in the Second Battle of Magh Tuiredh. Tethra appears in the verses associated with the magic of Amergin (see page 134):

> Who makes clear the ruggedness of the mountains?
> Who but myself knows where the sun shall set?
> Who foretells the ages of the moon?
> Who brings the cattle from the House of Tethra?
> On whom do the cattle of Tethra smile?
> Who shapes weapons from hill to hill?

The cattle of Tethra are of course fish, and in the verse the poet is claiming the skills and powers necessary for human survival, blessed by knowledge. Tethra is known as an Otherworld lord of the type who presides over a joyous assembly, one of the major themes of Celtic myth associated with a number of different gods.

The beauty of the undersea realm is described in the seventh-century *Voyage of Bran*:

> Sea horses glisten in summer
> As far as Bran's eye may see,
> Flowers pour forth as streams of honey
> In the land of Manannan mac Lir . . .
>
> Speckled salmon leap from the womb
> Of the white sea on which you look;
> They are calves, they are bright coloured lambs,
> At peace without strife.
>
> It is along the top of a forest
> That your tiny craft has sailed,
> A beautiful forest with its harvest of fruits
> Under the prow of your little boat.
>
> A wood with blossom and fruit
> And the true fragrance of the vine upon it,
> A wood without decay or death
> With leaves of golden colour . . .

Manannan was visualized riding his sea-chariot across the wave tops, or as riding the wave-horses. Significantly he is associated not only with the physical Isle of Man, but with Emain Abhlach, the Island of Apple Trees, said to be the Isle of Arran on the Firth of Clyde, but obviously an Otherworld location. This island is related to the Avalon of King Arthur, and the theme occurs again in the *Vita Merlini* of Geoffrey of Monmouth, where Merlin and the bard Taliesin take the wounded Arthur to the Fortunate Island to be cured of his deadly wound by the goddess Morgen, shape-changing mistress of therapy, music and the arts, co-ruling with her Nine Sisters. Significantly the ferryman for this journey is Barinthus, a mysterious character who echoes the role of the ancient sea gods, who 'knows well the way of sea and stars'.

It seems likely, from the character of Barinthus, that traditions of sea deities connected to the Otherworld paradise were preserved in British bardic tradition as late as the twelfth century, when Geoffrey was writing. Once again there is a comparison to be made between Geoffrey's work and that of the transcribers of the *Book of Invasions* and other Irish texts from oral tradition.

Geoffrey also makes one of the most famous references to a Celtic sea god, for he re-tells the mythic history of King Leir in his *History of the Kings of Britain*, a tale that was to be taken up and developed some centuries later by William Shakespeare, probably working from the *Chronicles* of Holinshed, which were in turn drawn from those of Geoffrey and a long line of interim chroniclers adapting successively from one another. Geoffrey's Leir was the son of King Bladud, who has all the attributes of a Celtic Druidic deity, but while Bladud was a god of the Underworld Sun, Leir (in Geoffrey) was associated with the river Soar in Leicestershire. Thus he is similar to those deities, such as Nodons, who were of both sea and river. The theme of three daughters fighting for the kingdom, developed so powerfully by Shakespeare, has all the hallmark of myth, as Celtic goddesses were frequently triplicated.

Thus we have Leir, son of a divine king (Bladud), who has in turn three daughters who divide the land between them; on the death of Leir his daughter Cordelia (according to Geoffrey) had him buried in an underground chamber beneath the river Soar. This chamber, to which all the craftsmen of the region used to come at the beginning of the year to perform their first act of labour, was dedicated to the god Janus.

Janus appears again in Geoffrey's version of the *Prophecies of Merlin* as presiding over the end of the solar system. He is, classically, the god of Gateways. We can follow the faint line of mythic connections between the god of Gateways, King Leir, originally an ancient sea-god, Barinthus, the Ferryman to the Otherworld Paradise, Manannan mac Lir, and the even more shadowy figure of Tethra, Lord of the Sea Cattle.

ELOQUENCE

Celtic gods and goddesses frequently epitomized the qualities that were so distinctive in Celtic society . . . many of which survive today. Inspiration, poetic skill, heroic valour, artistic and creative skills and, of course, eloquence of speech. This last skill features strongly in Celtic tradition, and reappears frequently in hero tales, folklore and medieval literature of Celtic origin in Ireland and Wales. There was, naturally, a Celtic god of eloquence.

One of the most famous and enigmatic classical descriptions of this deity was written in the second century AD by Lucian describing a Gaulish image of Ogmios, who, he says, was a type of Celtic Hercules. This in itself is curious, as Hercules was not known as a god of eloquence, but as a hero of strength and superhuman endurance and courage. The labours of Hercules, as defined in classical myth, have a certain affinity to stellar and seasonal patterns.

Ogmios carried a club and a bow, and there are a number of carvings from the Romano–Celtic period showing a typical Hercules figure, with massive muscles and huge club.

Ogmios, however, was an old man, bald and wrinkled, with dark sun-burned skin. From the tip of his tongue fine chains ran to the ears of happy mortals, who were drawn along by his power. While the club and bow are typical classical implements of the hero Hercules, the age and chains of eloquence are highly individual. A Celt from Gaul told Lucian that Ogmios was identified with

Hercules rather than Hermes (the classical god of eloquent and occasionally persuasive and lying speech), because Hercules was the stronger of the two gods. From this we may deduce that the Celtic god of eloquence was a powerful deity, able to impose his strength upon others, much in the manner that Hercules does so in classical myth. But there are further subtleties to Ogmios, and he is not a god of brute strength. While Hercules displayed native cunning at times, Ogmios was the god of the binding strength of poetry, of the power of the poetic word, charm, incantation or image.

In Ireland the god Oghma is the equivalent of Ogmios, and Ogma was known as *grianainech* or 'sun-face'. Oghma is also a strong champion, but most significantly he is credited with invention of Ogham, the Celtic alphabet. This system of writing, which seems, initially, to be based upon the Latin alphabet yet has certain unique characteristics as a mnemonic system which are un-Roman, is best known in the form of lines or cuts made upon the edges of stones or pieces of wood. Various stones inscribed with Ogham survive to this day, and there are (according to Professor Barry Fell[32]) even Ogham stones on the eastern seaboard of the USA.

The form of Ogham known to us seems to have developed fairly late, in the third or fourth centuries AD, but may incorporate an earlier magical alphabet. Such alphabets are found, in a confused form, in Irish and Welsh legend as processions of animals or trees, in a typically Celtic vision in which the orders of creation literally spell out the name of All Being. This type of myth is closely connected to that of the Divine Child, known as Mabon or Oenghus, or even as the young Merlin. There is, interestingly, a connection in this theme between Ogmios/Hercules and Mabon/Christ. In early Christian symbolism, the figure of Hercules sometimes takes the role now identified with Saint Christopher, and we see images of a burly hero carrying the Child of Light over the river.

The Celtic Ogmios or Oghma Sun-Face, a champion with the magical power of words to bind men to follow him, may have originally been a psychopomp or heroic guide of the spirits of the dead. When we consider the eloquent descriptions of the Celtic Otherworld, and the theme of a Champion ferrying the Child over the River (which was originally a cosmic creation myth, reflected by the passages of souls to the realm of the dead) we may have an insight into the nature of this Celtic god. As the Celtic 'Hercules' was a god of eloquence, we have the added inference that the strength of eloquence or poetic power brings the Child of Light into human awareness.

In addition to this, the association in Ireland of this god with a magical alphabet is important on two levels: firstly the alphabet of Ogham was used to bind, or to bespell, and is clearly described as being used by the hero Cuchulainn to bind the advancing armies of Queen Medbh. This magical binding power is a reflection of a deeper myth, in which the letters are the development or expansion of creation. Thus Ogmios is the god who both binds and liberates, who conducts the soul into other dimensions or between worlds. The symbolism of chains, binding and unbinding, arises in a number of early Celtic verses, connected with the liberation or imprisonment of a hero or god; the divine child

Horse harness decoration, third to fourth century BC, from Manerbio, northern Italy.

Mabon is described as one of the famous Prisoners of the Land of Britain who was eventually set free by a band of heroes.

THE DAGHDHA

The greatest of the Irish gods seems to have been the Daghdha. His name meant the 'Good God', and he was also known as the 'Great Father' and the 'Mighty One of Knowledge'. He seems to have been specifically associated with Druidism as the god of Wisdom, a primal father deity of tremendous power. Two of the potent Celtic magical and spiritual symbols were the special attributes of the Daghdha; the cauldron and the club or staff. These were to reappear in medieval literature as the Grail and Lance of Arthurian legend, but in Irish Druidic tradition they were more primal and pagan magical implements.

The cauldron conferred endless satisfaction, a perpetual supply of food, and there are implications that it provided, like the Grail, spiritual nourishment just as much as physical. That the Daghdha controlled the Cauldron shows him as a god of abundance and fertility; indeed, the spear or club and cauldron are the male and female implements in ritual magic, just as they are male and female organs of sexuality in the human body. The club of the Daghdha brought life with one end and death with the other, a clear statement of polarity and power. There is a Celtic god from Gaul called Sucullus or Sucellos, the 'Good Striker', who is shown as a mature male bearing a long-handled mallet; he may be a variant form of the Daghdha.

As is often the case with titanic or powerful father gods in early cultures, the Celts were not above making fun of the Daghdha. We find this ambivalent attitude to powerful deities throughout the ancient world; in classical Greece or Rome the most terrible goddesses were frequently known as 'good', and mystical or religious education occasionally took the form of *ludibrium* or 'silly tale' or 'game' that masked its inner power.

The gigantic powerful Daghdha is sometimes described as wearing short clothing that revealed his buttocks, and just before the Second Battle of Magh Tuiredh he was encouraged by the Fomhoire to eat a vast pitful of porridge. Following this gargantuan feast, which consisted of eighty cauldrons full of oats, milk and fat, stuffed with whole sheep, pigs and goats, the Daghdha made love to one of the Fomhoirean women, who was so impressed with his sexual prowess that she agreed to turn her magical powers against her own race.

In another tale, the Daghdha makes love to the Morrigan on the eve of Samhain, 1 November, the turning point of the Celtic year. He actually has intercourse with her while she stands astride the river Unius in Connaught, for she is the death goddess washing the ominous dead of a forthcoming battle. In this superficially lusty and bloodthirsty theme, we find a god of life mating with a goddess of death; it is a strong expression of the great universal forces, represented in anthropomorphic form for human understanding. It seems very likely that this coarse but vital tone ran through much of Celtic mythology, and we need to realize that it is naturally wedded with symbolism and poetry of great subtlety and beauty. There is no implication in Celtic tradition of our modern attitude to sexuality, and certainly no implication of pornography in the myths that employ sexual imagery.

Invasions, Manifestations, Divisions

Much of our material for Irish mythological tradition comes from the twelfth-century *Leabhar Gabhala Eireann* or *Book of Invasions*. This important text is paralleled in many ways by the twelfth-century British book the *History of the Kings of Britain* by Geoffrey of Monmouth. Both texts drew upon oral tradition fused with classical and Biblical material. Both sought to bring the divergent native traditions into line with an orthodox Christian history, from the creation of Adam to the arrival of the current race in the land. Both retained pagan and mythical history that is quite at odds with a Christian viewpoint.

Yet Christianity of the early centuries was different from that of the later medieval period, and within the dogma of the political church there seems also to have been leeway to accommodate the mass of beliefs of the people (which is to say, the mass of pagan beliefs and practices still active) in order to bring them into a Christian sphere of control. When we consider texts such as the *Book of Invasions* or the *History of the Kings of Britain*, we are not merely discovering relics of ancient tradition rendered as pseudo-Christian by cunning monastics; they represent the mixture of beliefs of the chroniclers themselves, who held oral tradition in great esteem. In other words there was not necessarily a mental conflict when sharing ancient bardic lore concerning the magical battles of the gods and ancestors with the teachings of the Bible.

It is in this atmosphere of fusion, of organic development of legend and religion, that we should consider medieval texts preserving traditions of Celtic gods and goddesses. Furthermore, we must remember that the deities represented skills and qualities in addition to superhuman or mysterious forces; ordinary people identified with the abilities of the gods and goddesses, and had a constant dialogue with such beings. We know this much not only from early pagan inscriptions from the Roman period, but from the thousands of beautiful prayers dedicated by the Celts to their saints; saints like Brigit, who is a thinly disguised pagan Celtic goddess. Such prayers and ritual formed part of the daily life of the 'Christian' Celts.

THE BOOK OF INVASIONS

The Irish *Book of Invasions* describes six waves of people or races arriving in Ireland, and attempts to merge its pagan tradition, originally derived from a lost Druidic mythical cycle of creation, with Christian pseudo-history.

Bull from Lille Bonne, France. Compare with example from Scotland on page 16.

The six waves or immigrations, the last one being that of the Gaels themselves, are treated as factual history, but seem to represent a cosmic sequence in which the appearance of certain types of being is synchronous with developments or phases of the creation of the world, typified by the land of Ireland. The first five races are:

1 Cessair
2 Partholon
3 Nemed
4 Fir Bolg
5 Tuatha De Danann.

The first race, led by Cessair, daughter of Bith the son of Noah, all perished in the Flood. They represent a very primal stage of creation which was destroyed: significantly the name Cessair is sometimes replaced by that of Banbha, one of the many names for the land of Ireland, an eponymous goddess or primal figure of Sovereignty.

After the Flood the sole survivor of this proto-race was Fintan, who passed through many animal shapes, enduring through the ages and surviving all the following invasions or phases of creation. Fintan, in early texts drawn from oral tradition, was magically invoked to describe the history of the land, and is described as the primal authority on Irish tradition. He is thus a prototype of the Druid who preserves all knowledge, but also echoes the perennial role of shaman or magician, who is able to obtain all knowledge through a cycle of relationship to totem animals. We find this theme repeated in the Welsh *Mabinogion* tale of Culhwch and Olwen and the Scots/Welsh legends of Merlin, as described in the *Vita Merlini*, where Merlin outlives the oldest animal of all, but before doing so passes through a series of totem animal relationships, including his phase as Lord of the Animals, identified with the Celtic god Cernunnos. Fintan, however, took the form of a salmon, an eagle and a hawk; we find such shape-changing themes in other Celtic Druidic sources.

Partholon and his tribe fought the first battle known in Ireland, their opponents being the *Fomhoire* or One-Eyed Beings of the Underworld. This development was also marked by the clearing of plains; in the time of Partholon four plains were cleared, and seven lakes appeared. Thus the land is become increasingly defined; forces of Above and Below exist in tension or conflict with one another, and the cardinal points of reference are established. Partholon is also cited as the originator of many skills and customs, such as the building of guest houses for hospitality (a very important aspect of Celtic social life), the brewing of ale and the establishing of certain basic laws. The people of Partholon were destroyed by plague.

Nemed led the third invasion of Ireland. The name is found in connection with sacred groves in Celtic religion, and is also known as the form of the Romano–Celtic goddess Nemetona: *nemed* or *nemeton* means a grove. It is tempting to see in this title or name the reflection of a Druidic ancestral myth, as the Druids were clearly associated with sacred groves and magical trees. Twelve plains were cleared during the rule of Nemed, and four lakes formed: the land or world became increasingly defined.

In the context of an increasingly defined pattern of creation, symbolized by the mythic history of the land, texts such as the *Book of Invasions* echo a number of other primal sources that deal with cosmic origins. The Four Plains and Seven Lakes of the time of Partholon, for example, are reminiscent of the Four Elements and Seven Powers or Seven Planets found in ancient classical cosmology and metaphysics; they may also represent four phases of manifestation, defined in esoteric or magical traditions as:

1 Origination out of the void
2 Creation of defined energies out of chaos
3 Formation of energies or forces into form, and
4 Expression as manifest universe, stars, worlds and living beings.

The subsequent development, in the time of Nemed, of twelve lakes and four plains is reminiscent of the zodiacal system of twelve Signs (and twelve Houses) and Four Elements, within which the Seven Planets move and interact.

While such an interpretation is purely speculative, we find astrological and cosmological lore in the parallel British texts set out from bardic tradition by Geoffrey of Monmouth. The *Prophecies of Merlin*, for example, more or less a contemporary of the *Book of Invasions*, contains many proto-astrological images, and describes a cosmology or manifesting land divided by three rivers (see page 66).

In the *Vita Merlini* a detailed cosmology is described, beginning with Four Original Powers, and concluding with the Land of Britain, orders of created beings, and the location of the Otherworld or Fortunate Island.

In the *Book of Invasions*, after the death of Nemed, the Fomhoire caused the people of Nemed to pay a heavy tribute of corn, milk and children, every year at the feast of Samhain (1 November). Eventually the people of Nemed rose up and fought their oppressors, but only thirty survived. Of these thirty, one remaining boat crew of a force that had invaded the island of the Fomhoire, a number went North, while the rest travelled to Greece. By these place names we may assume a mythical location or locations, for such rationalizations are common in medieval texts; Spain, for example, was long used in English folk tradition as a euphemism for Hell or the Otherworld, and many similar substitutions are found in Celtic lore, poetry and early texts.

Image of a Celtic god, probably the originator of the legendary flying king, Bladud, who is associated with Aquae Sulis and the Temple of Minerva in medieval texts. The wings, flaming hair and coiled serpents beneath the chin are clearly visible. This impressive carving formed the central figure of the pediment of the Temple of Sulis Minerva.

The following two invasions of Ireland derived from those two sets of people who had travelled North or to Greece. The Fir Bolg came from those who had travelled to Greece and multiplied there, and additional peoples of the Gailioin and the Fir Domhainn are also identified with this phase of invasion and settlement. The Fir Bolg found a land already created and defined and, as we might expect, are credited with the next stage of development, which is social: they devised the Four Provinces of Ulster, Leinster, Munster and Connaught, which symbolized the Four Directions or cardinal points, with Meath as a fifth unifying region in the centre, with the sacred Druidic location of Uisnech. The Fourfold Creation, with a central Fifth, is a pattern found worldwide in mythology and cosmology, and we find that the myth erupts into reality, for this pattern was historical and factual in Ireland for many centuries, and not merely a legendary history (see Figure A, page 14).

Kingship was instituted by the Fir Bolg, a most important sacro-magical role, in which the king related to the goddess of the land is order to bring health and vitality to the land and its people. Here we find legend echoing and interacting with history, for it reflects upon the warrior caste and aristocratic structure of later Celtic culture: the first and best king of Ireland was Eochaidh mac Erc, whose reign represented a perfect Golden Age of kingship; but he was also the first king to be slain by a weapon.

So we find myth and history merging and manifesting, for by this period of the legendary history, we can begin tentatively to identify stages of factual development of Irish culture.

The Tuatha De Danann, People of the Goddess Danu, came from the North (the other branch of the descendants of Nemed). North is traditionally the location of magic, the powers of the Otherworld, and has certain implications of stellar mythology. The Tuatha De Danann were skilled in Druidic lore and magic, and brought four major objects of power into Ireland:

1 The Sword of Nuadha (associated with the East)
2 The Spear of Lugh (South)
3 The Cauldron of the Daghdha (West)
4 The Stone of Fal (North).

The sword was deadly, and none could escape its blows; the spear conferred victory upon its user; the cauldron was a vessel of perpetual plenty and nourishment; the stone shrieked under the foot of the rightful king. Such 'king stones' are of considerable importance in Celtic tradition, and mark not only a formal location of the investiture of a king, but echo the prehistoric sacrificial rites practised in megalithic temples.

The stone located today in Westminster Abbey, upon which British rulers are crowned, is probably the one carried off from Scotland by Edward I in 1296. This was the original Stone of Scone, used for the installation and crowning of Scottish kings; some writers still maintain today that this stone was the sacred king stone from Tara in Ireland, brought to Scotland by the Dalriadic kings. Regardless of the origins of the stone, and the further debate that the Westminster stone may in any case be a substitution, Edward's looting of Scottish relics of kingship and other religious items was a firm declaration of conquest. Magically it is essential for the royal line of Britain to be installed upon the sacred stone, a tradition still upheld today. Certain standing stones in Britain are called 'King's

Bronze helmet decoration, a totem boar, first century BC, from Bata, Hungary.

Stone', one of the best known being part of the prehistoric complex of the Rollright Stones in Oxfordshire.

The Four Implements, sword, spear, cauldron and stone, all feature in Arthurian legend, and in harmonic forms as sword, rod, cup, and shield or mirror, are the implements of magical art to this day. Renaissance tarot cards, drawing from earlier traditions, represent the Four Elements of Air, Fire, Water and Earth, with sword, staff, cup and coins respectively; these became spades (swords), clubs (staffs/spears), hearts (cauldron/cups) and lozenges or diamonds (shields/stones/mirrors) in the deck of cards known today. Celtic magical traditions survive in many forms if we know how to trace them!

THE FIRST BATTLE OF MAGH TUIREDH

The Tuatha De Danann fought the Fir Bolg for the kingship, at the First Battle of Magh Tuiredh. The Fir Bolg lost, and the kingship passed to the Tuatha De Danann, but they were soon challenged by the ancient forces of opposition, the Fomhoire. In the battle the king of the Tuatha De Danann, Nuadha, had an arm cut off. He was later to have this replaced by a silver arm fashioned by Dian Cecht, the physician/smith, and so gain the title of Argetlam or Silver-Hand, but a maimed king could not rule under Celtic law, and replacement was sought for him. The people chose Bres the Beautiful, half Fomhoire and half of the Tuatha De; this joint parentage, with his father being of the Underworld Fomhoire and his mother of the Tuatha De Danann, is reminiscent of a number of Celtic themes in which a beautiful child has parentage in two worlds. The mysterious Mabon or Maponus, and Pryderi, of British tradition, and the youthful Merlin, have such parentage; children of two worlds were potent beings. We may see a hint of this theme in the begetting of King Arthur in the medieval legends, and perhaps inverted in the dark role of his incest-begotten nephew Mordred.

The rule of Bres was oppressive, and the Tuatha De Danann were reduced to the status of slaves. Bres was finally satirized for his mean nature and lack of hospitality by the poet Coirbre. The magical power of satire was dreaded by the ancient Celts, for a powerful poet could satirize a man and reduce him not only as a figure of ridicule, but in physical health and well-being. Bres was afflicted by the satire and the Tuatha De declared that he was no longer fit to be king; he assembled a host of Fomhoire to support his rule. Once again we find echoes of this theme in British legend, as if the tales of Arthur and his court are reworkings of Celtic themes that are found in more primal form in the Irish sources. Clearly a fundamental or primal tradition inspires both streams of legend.

At this point in the *Book of Invasions* Nuadha is fitted with his silver arm and restored to kingship, but upon the arrival of Lugh, master of all arts and crafts, at the royal court, the rulership is ceded to him. Celtic kingship was deeply related to ability and function, not to politics or primogeniture, though these later elements gradually suppressed the earlier magical traditions.

THE SECOND BATTLE OF MAGH TUIREDH

So the Tuatha De Danann fought the Fomhoire, and were led in the battle by Lugh, who seems to be the forerunner of the figure of Lancelot in later legends. The battle was fought with magical powers and wonderful weapons, and it is clear from the nature of these forces that we are encountering a conflict of energies connected to the sovereignty or well-being of the land, with a further implication of war or resolution of energies between other dimensions. The mountains of Ireland were used as weapons, and the lakes and rivers were concealed by the royal cupbearer from the enemy. Showers of fire were invoked by the Druids, and spells were cast to weaken the courage of the enemy.

The Tuatha De Danann had the added advantage of the therapeutic magic of Dian Cecht, who brought the dead back to life by immersion in a well and making incantations; this is a typical feature of Celtic religion, in which life and regeneration are found in wells, springs and underground sources. The final conflict was between Lugh and Balar of the Dreadful Eye; this terrible Fomhoire could destroy a host of men with his glance, but a slingshot from Lugh drove the eye out of the back of Balar's head, where it emitted its terrible energies upon the Fomhoire themselves.

After this battle, Bres was captured and the Fomhoire eventually banished from Ireland. Bres offered to ensure that the cattle were always in milk and there should be a harvest every quarter, but this offer was not acceptable. Finally his life was spared when he guaranteed to give advice on the proper times for ploughing, sowing and reaping. One of the themes that seems to be contained in this epic of cosmology and magical environmental symbolism is the fusion of the higher skills and crafts beloved of the Celts, such as poetry, magic, warrior skills, smithcraft and medicine, with the chthonic Underworld powers connected with fertility. With all their potent arts and skills, the Tuatha De Danann still had to grant Bres, the Fomhoire, his life, as they needed his advice on the fertility of the land.

THE HUMAN INVASION

The final race to arrive in Ireland, according to the *Book of Invasions*, were the Gaels, who landed in the south-west on Beltane or the first day of May. Although

The Ridgeway, leading to Wayland's Smithy. Such ancient ridge roads were in existence in Britain before the coming of the Romans.

the *Book of Invasions* is a pseudo-history, it reflects an ancient Celtic cosmology in which successive orders of beings appear through differing worlds, and finally the human race appears in the land. But in Celtic magic and religion, all the ancestors and earlier races are present either in other states or dimensions or reflecting through the spirit, soul and psyche of humans within the land. Hence the seeming confusion and intermingling of ages, beings, worlds and forces. Much of this confusion comes from the state of early literature, heavily edited and Christianized. Yet the chroniclers were attempting to modify, justify and preserve an oral bardic or Druidic tradition that was, to a certain extent, already in decline by the Middle Ages, though this decline was less apparent in Ireland. But we need not assume that there is, or ever was, a 'definitive order' to Celtic mythological cosmology, or gods and goddesses; the relationship is protean, organic, harmonic, not rigid or pre-determined.

The arrival of the Gaels, or of the human race, known as the Sons of Mil in Ireland, is declared by one of the most famous and beautiful of Celtic magical verses, uttered by the poet Amergin as he set his right foot upon the land; this poem is found also in Welsh versions, and was perhaps one of the major incantations or magical verses of the Druidic religion. The Gaels were said to have travelled from Spain, and an attempt was made to equate the name of Hibernia, Ireland, with Iberia or Spain. A similar attempt was made by Geoffrey of Monmouth in his *History*, rationalizing British Celtic lore, for he suggested that Britain was founded by Brutus, grandson of Aeneas, leading a troop of Trojans into the land. Just as the Irish races fought previous chthonic inhabitants of the land, so did Brutus and his warriors fight a band of giants in Cornwall, it is suggested, before being able to found their city of Troya Nova where London now stands.

Thus while the British were traditionally related to the Greeks or Trojans, the Irish were traditionally related to the Spaniards. Both relationships may have some factual basis, as there were Celtic populations in both Greece and Spain at an early date. The Spanish theme may be a rationalization of an older tradition in which humanity appeared from the Underworld.

The magical poem of Amergin, uttered as he set his right foot upon the land of Ireland, is a typical incantation, in which the poet or magician assumes the identity of the orders of creation within the new land:

I am a wind of the sea
I am a wave of the sea
I am the sound of the sea
I am a stag of seven tines [antlers]
I am a hawk on the cliff
I am a teardrop in the sun
I am the fairest of fair flowers
I am a raging boar
I am a salmon in a pool
I am a lake upon a fair plain
I am spear that roars for blood
I am the god of inspiring fire.

The Sons of Mil battled with the Tuatha De Danann and made their way to Tara, the seat of kingship for the land. As they travelled they met with three aspects of the goddess of Sovereignty of Ireland, Banbha, Eriu and Fodla. Thus we have a motif in which the goddess of the land greets incoming (or manifesting) peoples; Amergin promised Eriu that the land would bear her name as its first and main name, and she in turn declared that Ireland would belong to the Sons of Mil until the end of time. The Sons of Mil called upon the three original kings or consorts of the triple goddess at Tara to surrender the land and, after a ritualistic and magical contest, it was made clear that Amergin and his people had the blessing of the goddess. The chief of the Gaels, Donn, however, was drowned as a result of his discourtesy to the goddess ... yet we find him reappearing as shadowy god or primal ancestor living upon a distant western isle and summoning his people home at death. The support of the goddess was considered essential for kingship; the great Ulster hero Cuchulainn failed to recognize the war goddess, the Morrigan, so was deprived of her aid in battle; likewise Donn who failed to come to terms with the goddess of the land could no longer be leader of his people.

THE WORLD ABOVE AND THE WORLD BELOW

When the Sons of Mil, the Gaels or humans, defeated the Tuatha De Danann and become attuned to the Land of Ireland, the Tuatha remained powerful. By magical means they afflicted the growth of corn and production of milk, until a formal agreement was made between the two races or orders of being. The upper regions of the land became the realm of humans, while the lower regions, under the earth, became the realm of the Tuatha De Danann. To this day the *sidh* or fairy hills are found all over Ireland, and strong folk traditions preserve the knowledge of a mysterious people living underground. This tradition was also

strong in Scotland and persists in Gaelic-speaking regions even to the present day.

When the land was divided into upper and lower parts, the Daghdha allocated specific hills or mounds to each of the chieftains of the Tuatha De. Such mounds are sometimes natural hills, but many are the megalithic burial mounds and remains of the early pre-Celtic culture that spread across Britain and Ireland in the third millennium BC.

Thus we have a curious picture, a set of images that reflect one another in a progression: the early orders of being are replaced by later ones, until humanity appears. The pre-human divine or fairy race become rulers of the Underworld (originally the realm of the Fir Bolg or Fomhoireans, who were in turn conquered by the Tuatha De), but the physical mounds are the vast works of a prehistoric civilization, such as the Bruigh na Boinne, said to be the dwelling of Angus Og, the youthful god of love and death.

By the time this progression or series of reflections appears in the threshold texts of medieval literature, we find the divinity of the Tuatha De Danann is beginning to fade as a formal declaration, yet it persists quite clearly in their attributes and the traditions attached to them. A seventh-century biography of St Patrick mentions the *sidh* or gods of the earth. We find that the Welsh medieval legends of the *Mabinogion* describe an Underworld kingdom, over which a human rules in place of its Otherworldly king. Many mounds in Britain are associated with fairies or in-dwellers in folk tradition; in time the Celtic gods and goddesses become mingled with the ancestors – which is perhaps not surprising when we realize that the ancient burial mounds were indeed the last dwelling of ancestral people.

The immortality of the fairies, or people of the *sidh*, persisted in oral tradition well into the nineteenth century, when the concept of a deathless and beautiful Otherworld was rekindled in the work of poets and playwrights, though it had never been extinguished in the Celtic imagination. The fairy realm is the magical inverse of the human world; below to above, inside to outside. Time passes at a different rate in the Otherworld or land of the *sidh*; a brief visit can be hundreds of years in the human world.

Although the Christian churches banned formal worship of the old gods and goddesses, offerings were, and still are, left for the fairies or mound dwellers. A vast tradition of beliefs and practices connected to the people of the hollow hills exists in both Scotland and Ireland, and traces are found in Wales and Brittany of many similar practices. In Ireland it is supposedly St Patrick who halted worship of the Tuatha De Danann, but this was only the formal situation. Many Celtic prayers are concerned with averting the power of the fairies, for as time passed the religious propaganda increasingly coloured the mound dwellers as potentially harmful or malicious. It is interesting to note that they were not, generally, identified with devils or demons directly, though some propagandist themes suggest that the beauty and immortality of the *sidh* was due to paying fines to Hell every seven years.

Any attempt at truly understanding the Celtic gods and goddesses, mythology and magic must take into account the enduring and well-documented traditions of the Second Sight and the Fairy people. These are not intellectual assessments of historical patterns or remains, but the accounts of a living tradition among

Celtic people, of real experiences. Perhaps the most famous account is the Revd Robert Kirk's *Secret Commonwealth*[40], written in the seventeenth century, in which many incidents and beliefs concerning the Fairy world are set out as heard from Kirk's Gaelic-speaking parishioners. Although the material is coloured by religious orthodoxy, as we would expect, it is a remarkable account of the Second Sight and experiences associated with this ability. Most significantly Kirk cites that when Gaels emigrate to America or to Canada the Sight fades away, and he even suggests that it is tied in to the native land in some way. This is reminiscent of the concept of Sovereignty and the sacred Land, with its divine and semi-divine inhabitants that relate to human beings, as found in records of pagan Celtic religion and society. (For a detailed text and analysis of Kirk's *Secret Commonwealth* see *Robert Kirk: Walker Between Worlds* by R. J. Stewart, Element Books, 1990.)

Afterword

The Celtic gods and goddesses were inseparable from the land, taking on the nature of each region in which the Celts lived, while retaining their inherent functions that transcended locality. To try to see these deities and the forces that they embody in the same way as our ancestors would have done seems almost impossible, yet their vision is perhaps not so far removed as we might think.

Although we have talked in terms of personae and images, it seems more likely that the Celts saw the gods and goddesses as inherent firstly within the land, and secondly within themselves. So many of the deities, myths and magical or religious practices suggest this, that we cannot presume that the Celts worshipped their gods and goddesses as distant or impersonal forms devoid of intimate contact. Thus when we consider the flow of a river, the presence of a great tree, or the shape of a range of ancient hills, we are literally looking at the Celtic gods and goddesses inherent within the living land.

When we look within, in imagination, visualization or meditation, we are seeking for those forces within ourselves that were represented by the deities; for the Celtic gods and goddesses mediated skills, creative energies, inspiration, eloquence, prophecy and understanding of the forces of life and death. They were not images to which people bowed and sacrificed in order to propitiate or beg external influence upon their affairs, though concepts of cyclical patterns, polarity, rhythm and good or ill fortune were woven deeply into Celtic culture. Nor were the Celtic gods and goddesses seen as creators removed from their creation. They were never distant, never inaccessible; indeed, they were sometimes terrifyingly and uncomfortably close.

One of the problems of modern interest in ancient myths and legends, and in some of the modern ecological and revival pantheistic or pagan movements, is a degree of coyness, of cosy escapism and childish false security. Being *childish* is by no means the same as being *childlike*, and it is through the childlike and innocent qualities of the imagination that we may approach the old gods and goddesses, shedding our false sophistication and materialism. But to really shed such coverings and protections, to be really childlike and share the consciousness of our ancestors is to be open to both joy and terror, for the true nature of reality is not sweetened by the gods and goddesses, but made more accessible and intense to the aware.

The growing interest in ancient sites in Britain, Europe and the Americas is one of the strongest indications that people are seeking to regenerate a contact with the environmental and magical awareness of earlier cultures, to contact the Ancestors. This may be nothing more than a stroll around a popular monument, or it may be an intense experience alone at night in a sacred place, far from all the usual securities and toys of home. The Celts believed, and still believe, that you could step from one world to another in certain sacred places, and that humans, Otherworld beings, gods and goddesses, were able to meet face to face, or to exchange between each other's proper states and dimensions. If this is indeed true, and if our growing awareness of Celtic gods and goddesses and the sanctity of the environment is a genuine collective transformation, then we are in for interesting times.

Appendix:
Math, Son of Mathonwy

THIS IS THE FOURTH PORTION OF THE MABINOGION

Math the son of Mathonwy was lord over Gwynedd, and Pryderi the son of Pwyll was lord over the one-and-twenty Cantrevs of the South; and these were the seven Cantrevs of Dyved, and the seven Cantrevs of Morganwc, the four Cantrevs of Ceredigiawn, and the three of Ystrad Tywi.

At that time, Math the son of Mathonwy could not exist unless his feet were in the lap of a maiden, except only when he was prevented by the tumult of war. Now the maiden who was with him was Goewin, the daughter of Pebin of Dôl Pebin, in Arvon, and she was the fairest maiden of her time who was known there.

And Math dwelt always at Caer Dathyl, in Arvon, and was not able to go the circuit of the land, but Gilvaethwy the son of Don, and Eneyd the son of Don, his nephews, the sons of his sister, with his household, went the circuit of the land in his stead.

Now the maiden was with Math continually, and Gilvaethwy the son of Don set his affections upon her, and loved her so that he knew not what he should do because of her, and therefrom behold his hue, and his aspect, and his spirits changed for love of her, so that it was not easy to know him.

One day his brother Gwydion gazed steadfastly upon him. 'Youth,' said he, 'what aileth thee?' 'Why,' replied he, 'what seest thou in me?' 'I see,' said he, 'that thou hast lost thy aspect and thy hue; what, therefore, aileth thee?' 'My lord brother,' he answered, 'that which aileth me, it will not profit me that I should own to any.' 'What may it be, my soul?' said he. 'Thou knowest,' he said, 'that Math the son of Mathonwy has this property, that if men whisper together, in a tone how low soever, if the wind meet it, it becomes known unto him.' 'Yes,' said Gwydion, 'hold now thy peace, I know thy intent, thou lovest Goewin.'

When he found that his brother knew his intent, he gave the heaviest sigh in the world. 'Be silent, my soul, and sigh not,' he said. 'It is not thereby that thou wilt succeed. I will cause,' said he, 'if it cannot be otherwise, the rising of Gwynedd, and Powys, and Deheubarth, so seek the maiden. Be thou of glad cheer, therefore, and I will compass it.'

So they went unto Math the son of Mathonwy. 'Lord,' said Gwydion, 'I have heard that there have come to the South some beasts, such as were never known in this island before.' 'What are they called?' he asked. 'Pigs, lord.' 'And what kind of animals are they?' 'They are small animals, and their flesh is better than the flesh of oxen.' 'They are small, then?' 'And they change their names. Swine are they now called.' 'Who owneth them?' 'Pryderi the son of Pwyll; they were sent him from Annwn, by Arawn the king of Annwn, and still they keep that name, half hog, half pig.' 'Verily,' asked he, 'and by what means may they be obtained from him?' 'I will go, lord, as one of twelve, in the guise of bards, to seek the swine.' 'But it may be that he will refuse you,' said he. 'My journey will not be evil, lord,' said he; 'I will not come back without the swine.' 'Gladly,' said he, 'go thou forward.'

So he and Gilvaethwy went, and ten other men with them. And they came into Ceredigiawn, to the place that is now called Rhuddlan Teivi, where the palace of Pryderi was. In the guise of bards they came in, and they were received joyfully, and Gwydion was placed beside Pryderi that night.

'Of a truth,' said Pryderi, 'gladly would I have a tale from some of your men yonder.' 'Lord,' said Gwydion, 'we have a custom that the first night that we come to the Court of a great man, the chief of song recites. Gladly will I relate a tale.' Now Gwydion was the best teller of tales in the world, and he diverted all the Court that night with pleasant discourse and with tales, so that he charmed every one in the Court, and it pleased Pryderi to talk with him.

And after this, 'Lord,' said he unto Pryderi, 'were it more pleasing to thee, that another should discharge my errand unto thee, than that I should tell thee myself what it is?' 'No,' he answered, 'ample speech hast thou.' 'Behold then, lord,' said he, 'my errand. It is to crave from thee the animals that were sent thee from Annwn.' 'Verily,' he replied, 'that were the easiest thing in the world to grant, were there not a covenant between me and my land concerning them. And the covenant is that they shall not go from me, until they have produced double their number in the land.' 'Lord,' said he, 'I can set thee free from those words, and this is the way I can do so; give me not the swine to-night, neither refuse them unto me, and to-morrow I will show thee an exchange for them.'

And that night he and his fellows went unto their lodging, and they took counsel. 'Ah, my men,' said he, 'we shall not have the swine for the asking.' 'Well,' said they, 'how may they be obtained?' 'I will cause them to be obtained,' said Gwydion.

Then he betook himself to his arts, and began to work a charm. And he caused twelve chargers to appear, and twelve black greyhounds, each of them white-breasted, and having upon them twelve collars and twelve leashes, such as no one that saw them could know to be other than gold. And upon the horses twelve saddles, and every part which should have been of iron was entirely of gold, and the bridles were of the same workmanship. And with the horses and the dogs he came to Pryderi.

'Good day unto thee, lord,' said he. 'Heaven prosper thee,' said the other, 'and greetings be unto thee.' 'Lord,' said he, 'behold here is a release for thee from the word which thou spakest last evening concerning the swine; that thou wouldst neither give nor sell them. Thou mayest exchange them for that which is better. And I will give these twelve horses, all caparisoned as they are, with their saddles and their bridles, and these twelve greyhounds, with their collars and

'Hercules', from the main altar of Aquae Sulis. Hercules was a widespread Romano–Celtic god, possibly amalgamated with Ogmios or Oghma, the Celtic god of eloquence and enlightenment.

their leashes as thou seest, and the twelve gilded shields that thou beholdest yonder.' Now these he had formed of fungus. 'Well,' said he, 'we will take counsel.' And they consulted together, and determined to give the swine to Gwydion, and to take his horses and his dogs and his shields.

Then Gwydion and his men took their leave, and began to journey forth with the pigs. 'Ah, my comrades,' said Gwydion, 'it is needful that we journey with speed. The illusion will not last but from the one hour to the same to-morrow.'

And that night they journeyed as far as the upper part of Ceredigiawn, to the place which, from that cause, is called Mochdrev still. And the next day they took their course through Melenydd, and came that night to the town which is likewise for that reason called Mochdrev, between Keri and Arwystli. And thence they journeyed forward; and that night they came as far as that Commot in Powys, which also upon account thereof is called Mochnant, and there tarried they that night. And they journeyed thence to the Cantrev of Rhos, and the place where they were that night is still called Mochdrev.

'My men,' said Gwydion, 'we must push forward to the fastnesses of Gwynedd with these animals, for there is a gathering of hosts in pursuit of us.' So they journeyed on to the highest town of Arllechwedd, and there they made a sty for the swine, and therefore was the name of Creuwyryon given to that town. And after they had made the sty for the swine, they proceeded to Math the son of Mathonwy, at Caerdathyl. And when they came there, the country was rising. 'What news is there here?' asked Gwydion. 'Pryderi is assembling one-and-twenty Cantrevs to pursue after you,' answered they. 'It is marvellous that you should have journeyed so slowly.' 'Where are the animals whereof you went in quest?' said Math. 'They have had a sty made for them in the other Cantrev below,' said Gwydion.

Thereupon, lo, they heard the trumpets and the host in the land, and they arrayed themselves and set forward and came to Penardd in Arvon.

And at night Gwydion the son of Don, and Gilvaethwy his brother, returned to Caerdathyl; and Gilvaethwy took Math the son of Mathonwy's couch. And while he turned out the other damsels from the room discourteously, he made Gocwin unwillingly remain.

And when they saw the day on the morrow, they went back unto the place where Math the son of Mathonwy was with his host; and when they came there, the warriors were taking counsel in what district they should await the coming of Pryderi, and the men of the South. So they went in to the council. And it was resolved to wait in the strongholds of Gwynedd, in Arvon. So within the two Maenors they took their stand, Maenor Penardd and Maenor Coed Alun. And there Pryderi attacked them, and there the combat took place. And great was the slaughter on both sides; but the men of the South were forced to flee. And they fled unto the place which is still called Nantcall. And thither did they follow them, and they made a vast slaughter of them there, so that they fled again as far as the place called Dol Pen Maen, and there they halted and sought to make peace.

And that he might have peace, Pryderi gave hostages, Gwrgi Gwastra gave he and three-and-twenty others, sons of nobles. And after this they journeyed in peace even unto Traeth Mawr; but as they went on together towards Melenryd, the men on foot could not be restrained from shooting. Pryderi despatched unto Math an embassy to pray him to forbid his people, and to leave it between him and Gwydion the son of Don, for that he had caused all this. And the messengers came to Math. 'Of a truth,' said Math, 'I call Heaven to witness, if it be pleasing unto Gwydion the son of Don, I will so leave it gladly. Never will I compel any to go to fight but that we ourselves should do our utmost.'

'Verily,' said the messengers, 'Pryderi saith that it were more fair that the man who did him this wrong should oppose his own body to his, and let his people remain unscathed.' 'I declare to Heaven, I will not ask the men of Gwynedd to fight because of me. If I am allowed to fight Pryderi myself, gladly will I oppose my body to his.' And this answer they took back to Pryderi. 'Truly,' said Pryderi, 'I shall require no one to demand my rights but myself.'

Then these two came forth and armed themselves, and they fought. And by force of strength, and fierceness, and by the magic and charms of Gwydion, Pryderi was slain. And at Maen Tyriawc, above Melenryd, was he buried, and there is his grave.

And the men of the South set forth in sorrow towards their own land; nor is it a marvel that they should grieve, seeing that they had lost their lord, and many of their best warriors, and for the most part their horses and their arms.

The men of Gwynedd went back joyful and in triumph. 'Lord,' said Gwydion unto Math, 'would it not be right for us to release the hostages of the men of the South, which they pledged unto us for peace, for we ought not to put them in prison?' 'Let them then be set free,' saith Math. So that youth, and the other hostages that were with him, were set free to follow the men of the South.

Math himself went forward to Caerdathyl. Gilvaethwy the son of Don, and they of the household that were with him, went to make the circuit of Gwynedd as they were wont, without coming to the Court. Math went into his chamber, and caused a place to be prepared for him whereon to recline, so that he might put his feet in the maiden's lap. 'Lord,' said Goewin, 'seek now another to hold thy feet, for I am now a wife.' 'What meaneth this?' said he. 'An attack, lord, was made unawares upon me; but I held not my peace, and there was no one in the Court who knew not of it. Now the attack was made by thy nephews, lord, the sons of thy sister, Gwydion the son of Don, and Gilvaethwy the son of Don; unto me they did wrong, and unto thee dishonour.' 'Verily,' he exclaimed, 'I will do to the utmost of my power concerning this matter. But first I will cause thee to have compensation, and then will I have amends made unto myself. As for thee, I will take thee to be my wife, and the possession of my dominions will I give unto thy hands.'

And Gwydion and Gilvaethwy came not near the Court, but stayed in the confines of the land until it was forbidden to give them meat and drink. At first they came not near unto Math, but at the last they came. 'Lord,' said they, 'Good day to thee.' 'Well,' said he, 'is it to make me compensation that ye are come?' 'Lord,' they said, 'we are at thy will.' 'By my will I would not have lost my warriors, and so many arms as I have done. You cannot compensate me my shame, setting aside the death of Pryderi. But since ye come hither to be at my will, I shall begin your punishment forthwith.'

Then he took his magic wand, and struck Gilvaethwy, so that he became a deer, and he seized the other lest he should escape from him. And he struck him with the same wand, and he became a deer also. 'Since now ye are in bonds, I will that ye go forth together and be companions, and possess the nature of the animals whose form ye bear. And this day twelvemonth come hither unto me.'

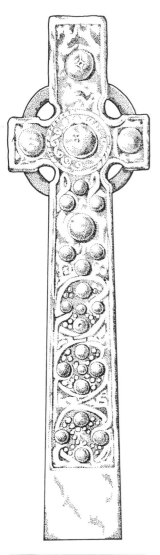

Celtic Christian cross from Iona, showing the symbols of the interwoven spheres or worlds.

At the end of a year from that day, lo there was a loud noise under the chamber wall, and the barking of the dogs of the palace together with the noise. 'Look,' said he, 'what is without.' 'Lord,' said one, 'I have looked; there are there two deer, and a fawn with them.' Then he arose and went out. And when he came he beheld the three animals. And he lifted up his wand. 'As ye were deer last year, be ye wild hogs each and either of you, for the year that is to come.' And thereupon he struck them with the magic wand. 'The young one will I take and cause to be baptized.' Now the name that he gave him was Hydwn. 'Go ye and be wild swine, each and either of you, and be ye of the nature of wild swine. And this day twelvemonth be ye here under the wall.'

At the end of the year the barking of dogs was heard under the wall of the chamber. And the Court assembled, and thereupon he arose and went forth, and when he came forth he beheld three beasts. Now these were the beasts that he saw; two wild hogs of the woods, and a well-grown young one with them. And he was very large for his age. 'Truly,' said Math, 'this one will I take and cause to be baptized.' And he struck him with his magic wand, and he became a fine fair auburn-haired youth, and the name that he gave him was Hychdwn. 'Now as for you, as ye were wild hogs last year, be ye wolves each and either of you for the year that is to come.' Thereupon he struck them with his magic wand, and they became wolves. 'And be ye of like nature with the animals whose semblance ye bear, and return here this day twelvemonth beneath this wall.'

And at the same day at the end of the year, he heard a clamour and a barking of dogs under the wall of the chamber. And he rose and went forth. And when he came, behold, he saw two wolves, and a strong cub with them. 'This one will I take,' said Math, 'and I will cause him to be baptized; there is a name prepared for him, and that is Bleiddwn. Now these three, such are they:

The three sons of Gilvaethwy the false,
The three faithful combatants,
Bleiddwn, Hydwn, and Hychdwn the Tall.'

Then he struck the two with his magic wand, and they resumed their own nature. 'Oh men,' said he, 'for the wrong that ye did unto me sufficient has been your punishment and your dishonour. Prepare now precious ointment for these men, and wash their heads, and equip them.' And this was done.

And after they were equipped, they came unto him. 'Oh men,' said he, 'you have obtained peace, and you shall likewise have friendship. Give your counsel unto me, what maiden I shall seek.' 'Lord,' said Gwydion the son of Don, 'it is easy to give thee counsel; seek Arianrod, the daughter of Don, thy niece, thy sister's daughter.'

And they brought her unto him, and the maiden came in. 'Ha, damsel,' said he, 'art thou a maiden?' 'I know not, lord, other than that I am.' Then he took up his magic wand, and bent it. 'Step over this,' said he, 'and I shall know if thou art a maiden.' Then stepped she over the magic wand, and there appeared forthwith a fine chubby yellow-haired boy. And at the crying out of the boy, she went towards the door. And thereupon some small form was seen; but before any one could get a second glimpse of it, Gwydion had taken it, and had flung a scarf of velvet around it and hidden it. Now the place where he hid it was the bottom of a chest at the foot of his bed.

'Verily,' said Math the son of Mathonwy, concerning the fine yellow-haired boy, 'I will cause this one to be baptized, and Dylan is the name I will give him.'

So they had the boy baptized, and as they baptized him he plunged into the sea. And immediately when he was in the sea, he took its nature, and swam as well as the best fish that was therein. And for that reason was he called Dylan, the son of the Wave. Beneath him no wave ever broke. And the blow whereby he came to his death, was struck by his uncle Govannion. The third fatal blow was it called.

As Gwydion lay one morning on his bed awake, he heard a cry in the chest at his feet; and though it was not loud, it was such that he could hear it. Then he arose in haste, and opened the chest; and when he opened it, he beheld an infant boy stretching out his arms from the folds of the scarf, and casting it aside. And he took up the boy in his arms, and carried him to a place where he knew there was a woman that could nurse him. And he agreed with the woman that she should take charge of the boy. And that year he was nursed.

And at the end of the year he seemed by his size as though he were two years old. And the second year he was a big child, and able to go to the Court by himself. And when he came to the Court, Gwydion noticed him, and the boy became familiar with him, and loved him better than any one else. Then was the boy reared at the Court until he was four years old, when he was as big as though he had been eight.

And one day Gwydion walked forth, and the boy followed him, and he went to the Castle of Arianrod, having the boy with him; and when he came into the Court, Arianrod arose to meet him, and greeted him and bade him welcome. 'Heaven prosper thee,' said he. 'Who is the boy that followeth thee?' she asked. 'This youth, he is thy son,' he answered. 'Alas,' said she, 'what has come unto thee that thou shouldst shame me thus; wherefore dost thou seek my dishonour, and retain it so long as this?' 'Unless thou suffer dishonour greater than that of my bringing up such a boy as this, small will be thy disgrace.' 'What is the name of the boy?' said she. 'Verily,' he replied, 'he has not yet a name.' 'Well,' she said, 'I lay this destiny upon him, that he shall never have a name until he receives one from me.' 'Heaven bears me witness,' answered he, 'that thou art a wicked woman. But the boy shall have a name, how displeasing soever it may be unto thee. As for thee, that which afflicts thee is that thou art no longer called a maiden.' And thereupon he went forth in wrath, and returned to Caer Dathyl, and there he tarried that night.

And the next day he arose and took the boy with him, and went to walk on the sea-shore between that place and Aber Menei. And there he saw some sedges and sea-weed, and he turned them into a boat. And out of dry sticks and sedges he made some Cordovan leather, and a great deal thereof, and he coloured it in such a manner that no one ever saw leather more beautiful than it. Then he made a sail to the boat, and he and the boy went in it to the port of the castle of Arianrod. And he began forming shoes and stitching them, until he was observed from the castle. And when he knew that they of the castle were observing him, he disguised his aspect, and put another semblance upon himself, and upon the boy, so that they might not be known. 'What men are those in yonder boat?' said Arianrod. 'They are cordwainers,' answered they. 'Go and see what kind of leather they have, and what kind of work they can do.'

So they came unto them. And when they came he was colouring some Cordovan leather, and gilding it. And the messengers came and told her this.

The Whispering Knights, the remains of a dolmen or capped chamber in the ritual complex of the Rollright Stones, Oxfordshire. In Celtic mythology such chambers were said to be the dwellings of the elder gods, later to become known as Fairies, or in Ireland as the people of the *sidh* or mounds. Although such megalithic monuments are associated with the Druids in popular belief, there is no hard evidence that they were actively used by the Celts. The Druids worshipped in tree groves, but it seems likely that seers, magicians and followers of the Dark Goddess might have used megalithic temples of sacred stones, and it is from this pre-Celtic level of religion that the associations between sacred kingship and stones derive.

'Well,' said she, 'take the measure of my foot, and desire the cordwainer to make shoes for me.' So he made the shoes for her, yet not according to the measure, but larger. The shoes then were brought unto her, and behold they were too large. 'These are too large,' said she, 'but he shall receive their value. Let him also make some that are smaller than they.' Then he made her others that were much smaller than her foot, and sent them unto her. 'Tell him that these will not go on my feet,' said she. And they told him this. 'Verily,' said he, 'I will not make her any shoes, unless I see her foot.' And this was told unto her. 'Truly,' she answered, 'I will go unto him.'

So she went down to the boat, and when she came there, he was shaping shoes and the boy stitching them. 'Ah, lady,' said he, 'good day to thee.' 'Heaven prosper thee,' said she. 'I marvel that thou canst not manage to make shoes according to a measure.' 'I could not,' he replied, 'but now I shall be able.'

Thereupon behold a wren stood upon the deck of the boat, and the boy shot at it, and hit it in the leg between the sinew and the bone. Then she smiled. 'Verily,' said she, 'with a steady hand did the lion aim at it.' 'Heaven reward thee not, but now has he got a name. And a good enough name it is. Llew Llaw Gyffes be he called henceforth.'

Then the work disappeared in sea-weed and sedges, and he went on with it no further. And for that reason was he called the third Gold-shoemaker. 'Of a truth,' said she, 'thou wilt not thrive the better for doing evil unto me.' 'I have done thee no evil yet,' said he. Then he restored the boy to his own form. 'Well,' said she, 'I will lay a destiny upon this boy, that he shall never have arms and armour until I invest him with them.' 'By Heaven,' said he, 'let thy malice be what it may, he shall have arms.'

Then they went towards Dinas Dinnllev, and there he brought up Llew Llaw

147

Gyffes, until he could manage any horse, and he was perfect in features, and strength, and stature. And then Gwydion saw that he languished through the want of horses, and arms. And he called him unto him. 'Ah, youth,' said he, 'we will go to-morrow on an errand together. Be therefore more cheerful than thou art.' 'That I will,' said the youth.

Next morning, at the dawn of day, they arose. And they took way along the sea coast, up towards Bryn Aryen. And at the top of Cevn Clydno they equipped themselves with horses, and went towards the Castle of Arianrod. And they changed their form, and pricked towards the gate in the semblance of two youths, but the aspect of Gwydion was more staid than that of the other. 'Porter,' said he, 'go thou in and say that there are here bards from Glamorgan.' And the porter went in. 'The welcome of Heaven be unto them, let them in,' said Arianrod.

With great joy were they greeted. And the hall was arranged, and they went to meat. When meat was ended, Arianrod discoursed with Gwydion of tales and stories. Now Gwydion was an excellent teller of tales. And when it was time to leave off feasting, a chamber was prepared for them, and they went to rest.

In the early twilight Gwydion arose, and he called unto him his magic and his power. And by the time that the day dawned, there resounded through the land uproar, and trumpets, and shouts. When it was now day, they heard a knocking at the door of the chamber, and therewith Arianrod asking that it might be opened. Up rose the youth and opened unto her, and she entered and a maiden with her. 'Ah, good men,' she said, 'in evil plight are we.' 'Yes, truly,' said Gwydion, 'we have heard trumpets and shouts; what thinkest thou that they may mean?' 'Verily,' said she, 'we cannot see the colour of the ocean by reason of all the ships side by side. And they are making for the land with all the speed they can. And what can we do?' said she. 'Lady,' said Gwydion, 'there is none other counsel than to close the castle upon us, and to defend it as best we may.' 'Truly,' said she, 'may Heaven reward you. And do you defend it. And here may you have plenty of arms.'

And thereupon went she forth for the arms, and behold she returned, and two maidens, and suits of armour for two men, with her. 'Lady,' said he, 'do thou accoutre this stripling, and I will arm myself with the help of thy maidens. Lo, I hear the tumult of the men approaching.' 'I will do so gladly.' So she armed him fully, and that right cheerfully. 'Hast thou finished arming the youth?' said he. 'I have finished,' she answered. 'I likewise have finished,' said Gwydion. 'Let us now take off our arms, we have no need of them.' 'Wherefore?' said she. 'Here is the army around the house.' 'Oh, lady, there is here no army.' 'Oh,' cried she, 'whence then was this tumult?' 'The tumult was but to break thy prophecy and to obtain arms for thy son. And now has he got arms without any thanks unto thee.' 'By Heaven,' said Arianrod, 'thou art a wicked man. Many a youth might have lost his life through the uproar thou hast caused in this Cantrev to-day. Now will I lay a destiny upon this youth,' she said, 'that he shall never have a wife of the race that now inhabits this earth.' 'Verily,' said he, 'thou wast ever a malicious woman, and no one ought to support thee. A wife shall he have notwithstanding.'

They went thereupon unto Math the son of Mathonwy, and complained unto him most bitterly of Arianrod. Gwydion showed him also how he had procured arms for the youth. 'Well,' said Math, 'we will seek, I and thou, by charms and illusion, to form a wife for him out of flowers. He has now come to man's stature, and he is the comeliest youth that was ever beheld.' So they took the blossoms of the meadow-sweet, and produced from them a maiden, the fairest and most graceful that man ever saw. And they baptized her, and gave her the name of Blodeuwedd.*

After she had become his bride, and they had feasted, said Gwydion, 'It is not easy for a man to maintain himself without possessions.' 'Of a truth,' said Math, 'I will give the young man the best Cantrev to hold.' 'Lord,' said he, 'what Cantrev is that?' 'The Cantrev of Dinodig,' he answered. Now it is called at this day Eivionydd and Ardudwy. And the place in the Cantrev where he dwelt, was a palace of his in a spot called Mur y Castell, on the confines of Ardudwy. There dwelt he and reigned, and both he and his sway were beloved by all.

One day he went forth to Caer Dathyl, to visit Math the son of Mathonwy. And on the day that he set out for Caer Dathyl, Blodeuwedd walked in the court. And she heard the sound of a horn. And after the sound of the horn, behold a tired stag went by, with dogs and huntsmen following it. And after the dogs and the huntsmen there came a crowd of men on foot. 'Send a youth,' said she, 'to ask who yonder host may be.' So a youth went and inquired who they were. 'Gronw Pebyr is this, the lord of Penllynn,' said they. And thus the youth told her.

Gronw Pebyr pursued the stag, and by the river Cynvael he overtook the stag and killed it. And what with flaying the stag and baiting his dogs, he was there until the night began to close in upon him. And as the day departed and the night drew near, he came to the gate of the Court. 'Verily,' said Blodeuwedd, 'the Chieftain will speak ill of us if we let him at this hour depart to another land without inviting him in.' 'Yes, truly, lady,' said they, 'it will be most fitting to invite him.'

Then went messengers to meet him and bid him in. And he accepted her bidding gladly, and came to the Court, and Blodeuwedd went to meet him and greeted him, and bade him welcome. 'Lady,' said he, 'Heaven repay thee thy kindness.'

When they had disaccoutred themselves, they went to sit down. And Blodeuwedd looked upon him, and from the moment that she looked on him she became filled with his love. And he gazed on her, and the same thought came unto him as unto her, so that he could not conceal from her that he loved her, but he declared unto her that he did so. Thereupon she was very joyful. And all their discourse that night was concerning the affection and love which they felt one for the other, and which in no longer space than one evening had arisen. And that evening passed they in each other's company.

The next day he sought to depart. But she said, 'I pray thee go not from me to-day.' And that night he tarried also. And that night they consulted by what means they might always be together. 'There is none other counsel,' said he, 'but that thou strive to learn from Llew Llaw Gyffes in what manner he will meet his death. And this must thou do under the semblance of solicitude concerning him.'

The next day Gronw sought to depart. 'Verily,' said she, 'I will counsel thee not to go from me to-day.' 'At thy instance will I not go,' said he, 'albeit, I must say, there is danger that the chief who owns the palace may return home.' 'To-morrow,' answered she, 'will I indeed permit thee to go forth.'

* Flower-face.

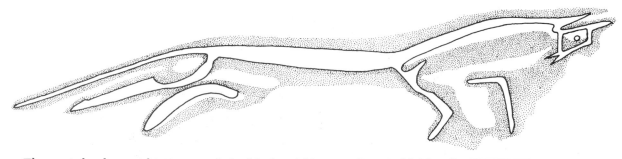

The next day he sought to go, and she hindered him not. 'Be mindful,' said Gronw, 'of what I have said unto thee, and converse with him fully, and that under the guise of the dalliance of love, and find out by what means he may come to his death.'

That night Llew Llaw Gyffes returned to his home. And the day they spent in discourse, and minstrelsy, and feasting. And at night they went to rest, and he spoke to Blodeuwedd once, and he spoke to her a second time. But, for all this, he could not get from her one word. 'What aileth thee,' said he, 'art thou well?' 'I was thinking,' said she, 'of that which thou didst never think of concerning me; for I was sorrowful as to thy death, lest thou shouldst go sooner than I.' 'Heaven reward thy care for me,' said he, 'but until Heaven take me I shall not easily be slain.' 'For the sake of Heaven, and for mine, show me how thou mightest be slain. My memory in guarding is better than thine.' 'I will tell thee gladly,' said he. 'Not easily can I be slain, except by a wound. And the spear wherewith I am struck must be a year in the forming. And nothing must be done towards it except during the sacrifice on Sundays.' 'Is this certain?' asked she. 'It is in truth,' he answered. 'And I cannot be slain within a house, nor without. I cannot be slain on horseback nor on foot.' 'Verily,' said she, 'in what manner then canst thou be slain?' 'I will tell thee,' said he. 'By making a bath for me by the side of a river, and by putting a roof over the cauldron, and thatching it well and tightly, and bringing a buck, and putting it beside the cauldron. Then if I place one foot on the buck's back, and the other on the edge of the cauldron, whosoever strikes me thus will cause my death.' 'Well,' said she, 'I thank Heaven that it will be easy to avoid this.'

No sooner had she held this discourse than she sent to Gronw Pebyr. Gronw toiled at making the spear, and that day twelvemonth it was ready. And that very day he caused her to be informed thereof.

'Lord,' said Blodeuwedd unto Llew, 'I have been thinking how it is possible that what thou didst tell me formerly can be true; wilt thou show me in what manner thou couldst stand at once upon the edge of a cauldron and upon a buck, if I prepare the bath for thee?' 'I will show thee,' said he.

Then she sent unto Gronw, and bade him be in ambush on the hill which is now called Bryn Cyvergyr, on the bank of the river Cynvael. She caused also to be collected all the goats that were in the Cantrev, and had them brought to the other side of the river, opposite Bryn Cyvergyr.

And the next day she spoke thus. 'Lord,' said she, 'I have caused the roof and the bath to be prepared, and lo! they are ready,' 'Well,' said Llew, 'we will go gladly to look at them.'

The day after they came and looked at the bath. 'Wilt thou go into the bath,

The Uffington White Horse, possibly cut into the chalk by the tribe of the Belgae in the first century BC, as a totem of the Horse Goddess.

The goddess Luna, from the temple of Sulis Minerva, Bath, England.

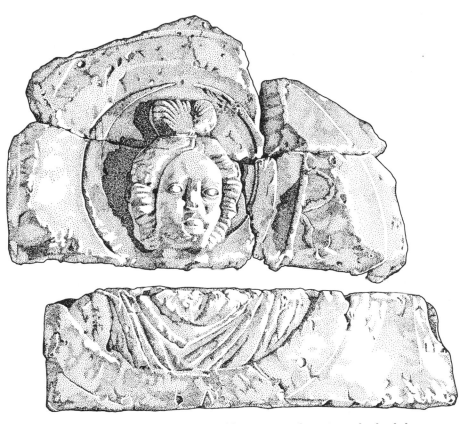

lord? 'said she. 'Willingly will I go in,' he answered. So into the bath he went, and he anointed himself. 'Lord,' said she, 'behold the animals which thou didst speak of as being called bucks.' 'Well,' said he, 'cause one of them to be caught and brought here.' And the buck was brought. Then Llew rose out of the bath, and he placed one foot on the edge of the bath and the other on the buck's back.

Thereupon Gronw rose up from the hill which is called Bryn Cyvergyr, and he rested on one knee, and flung the poisoned dart and struck him on the side, so that the shaft started out, but the head of the dart remained in. Then Llew flew up in the form of an eagle and gave a fearful scream. And thenceforth was he no more seen.

As soon as he departed Gronw and Blodeuwedd went together unto the palace that night. And the next day Gronw arose and took possession of Ardudwy. And after he had overcome the land, he ruled over it, so that Ardudwy and Penllyn were both under his sway.

Then these tidings reached Math the son of Mathonwy. And heaviness and grief came upon Math, and much more upon Gwydion than upon him. 'Lord,' said Gwydion, 'I shall never rest until I have tidings of my nephew.' 'Verily,' said Math, 'may Heaven be thy strength.' Then Gwydion set forth and began to go forward. And he went through Gwynedd and Powys to the confines. And when he had done so, he went into Arvon, and came to the house of a vassal, in Maenawr Penardd. And he alighted at the house, and stayed there that night. The man of the house and his household came in, and last of all came there the swineherd. Said the man of the house to the swineherd, 'Well, youth, hath thy sow come in to-night?' 'She hath,' said he, 'and is this instant returned to the pigs.' 'Where doth this sow go to?' said Gwydion. 'Every day, when the sty is opened, she goeth forth and none can catch sight of her, neither is it known whither she goeth more than if she sank into the earth.' 'Wilt thou grant unto me,' said Gwydion, 'not to open the sty until I am beside the sty with thee?' 'This will I do, right gladly,' he answered.

That night they went to rest; and as soon as the swineherd saw the light of day, he awoke Gwydion. And Gwydion arose and dressed himself, and went with the swineherd, and stood beside the sty. Then the swineherd opened the sty. And as soon as he opened it, behold she leaped forth, and set off with great speed. And Gwydion followed her, and she went against the course of a river, and made for a brook, which is now called Nant y Llew. And there she halted and began feeding. And Gwydion came under the tree, and looked what it might be that the sow was feeding on. And he saw that she was eating putrid flesh and vermin. Then looked he up to the top of the tree, and as he looked he beheld on the top of the tree an eagle, and when the eagle shook itself, there fell vermin and putrid flesh from off it, and these the sow devoured. And it seemed to him that the eagle was Llew. And he sang an Englyn:

'Oak that grows between the two banks;
Darkened is the sky and hill!
Shall I not tell him by his wounds,
That this is Llew?'

Upon this the eagle came down until he reached the centre of the tree. And Gwydion sang another Englyn:

'Oak that grows in upland ground,
Is it not wetted by the rain? Has it not been drenched
By nine score tempests?
It bears in its branches Llew Llaw Gyffes.'

Then the eagle came down until he was on the lowest branch of the tree, and thereupon this Englyn did Gwydion sing:

'Oak that grows beneath the steep;
Stately and majestic is its aspect!
Shall I not speak it?
That Llew will come to my lap?'

And the eagle came down upon Gwydion's knee. And Gwydion struck him with his magic wand, so that he returned to his own form. No one ever saw a more piteous sight, for he was nothing but skin and bone.

Then he went unto Caer Dathyl, and there were brought unto him good physicians that were in Gwynedd, and before the end of the year he was quite healed.

'Lord,' said he unto Math the son of Mathonwy, 'it is full time now that I have retribution of him by whom I have suffered all this woe.' 'Truly,' said Math, 'he will never be able to maintain himself in the possession of that which is thy right.' 'Well,' said Llew, 'the sooner I have my right, the better shall I be pleased.'

Then they called together the whole of Gwynedd, and set forth to Ardudwy.

And Gwydion went on before and proceeded to Mur y Castell. And when Blodeuwedd heard that he was coming, she took her maidens with her, and fled to the mountains. And they passed through the river Cynvael, and went towards a court that there was upon the mountain, and through fear they could not proceed except with their faces looking backwards, so that unawares they fell into the lake. And they were all drowned except Blodeuwedd herself, and her Gwydion overtook. And he said unto her, 'I will not slay thee, but I will do unto thee worse than that. For I will turn thee into a bird; and because of the shame thou hast done unto Llew Llaw Gyffes, thou shalt never show thy face in the light of day henceforth; and that through fear of all the other birds. For it shall be their nature to attack thee, and to chase thee from wheresoever they may find thee. And thou shalt not lose thy name, but shalt be always called Blodeuwedd.' Now Blodeuwedd is an owl in the language of this present time, and for this reason is the owl hateful unto all birds. And even now the owl is called Blodeuwedd.

Then Gronw Pebyr withdrew unto Penllyn, and he despatched thence an embassy. And the messengers he sent asked Llew Llaw Gyffes, if he would take land, or domain, or gold, or silver, for the injury he had received. 'I will not, by my confession to Heaven,' said he. 'Behold this is the least that I will accept from him; that he come to the spot where I was when he wounded me with the dart, and that I stand where he did, and that with a dart I take my aim at him. And this is the very least that I will accept.'

And this was told unto Gronw Pebyr. 'Verily,' said he, 'is it needful for me to do thus? My faithful warriors, and my household, and my foster-brothers, is there not one among you who will stand the blow in my stead?' 'There is not, verily,' answered they. And because of their refusal to suffer one stroke for their lord, they are called the third disloyal tribe even unto this day. 'Well,' said he, 'I will meet it.'

Then they two went forth to the banks of the river Cynvael, and Gronw stood in the place where Llew Llaw Gyffes was when he struck him, and Llew in the place where Gronw was. Then said Gronw Pebyr unto Llew, 'Since it was through the wiles of a woman that I did unto thee as I have done, I adjure thee by Heaven to let me place between me and the blow the slab thou seest yonder on the river's bank.' 'Verily,' said Llew, 'I will not refuse thee this.' 'Ah,' said he, 'may Heaven reward thee.' So Gronw took the slab and placed it between him and the blow.

Then Llew flung the dart at him, and it pierced the slab and went through Gronw likewise, so that it pierced through his back. And thus was Gronw Pebyr slain. And there is still the slab on the bank of the river Cynvael, in Ardudwy, having the hole through it. And therefore is it even now called Llech Gronw. A second time did Llew Llaw Gyffes take possession of the land, and prosperously did he govern it. And as the story relates, he was lord after this over Gwynedd.

AND THUS ENDS THIS PORTION OF THE MABINOGION.

(Translated by Lady Charlotte Guest)

Notes on Further Reading

FOOTNOTE NUMBERS REFER TO THE TEXTS LISTED BELOW.

Note: THE FOLLOWING IS A GENERAL LIST OF SELECTED TITLES FOR FURTHER READING ON SUBJECTS INDICATED IN EACH CHAPTER. IT IS NOT BY ANY MEANS A FULL BIBLIOGRAPHY OF CELTIC MYTHOLOGY AND RELATED SUBJECTS, BUT MANY OF THE BOOKS LISTED BELOW CARRY EXTENSIVE BIBLIOGRAPHIES FOR FURTHER STUDY AND PLEASURE.

1 Guest, Lady C. (trans., with notes by Alfred Nutt), *The Mabinogion*, Alfred Nutt, London 1904. Also trans. J. Gantz, Penguin, Harmondsworth 1976.
Matthews, C., *Mabon and the Mysteries of Britain*, Arkana, London 1987.

2 Stewart, R.J., *The Prophetic Vision of Merlin*, Arkana, London 1986. Includes translation and commentary upon the *Prophecies of Merlin* of 1135, by Geoffrey of Monmouth.
Stewart, R.J. (ed.), *The Second Book of Merlin* (papers from the annual Merlin Conference by various authors), Blandford Press, London 1988.

3 Graves, R., *The Greek Myths* (2 vols.), Penguin, Harmondsworth, 1964.

4 Stewart, R.J., *Where is Saint George?*, Blandford Press, London 1988. Pagan imagery in English folksong (reprint of 1976 edition).
Rawe, R., *Padstow's Obby Oss*, R. Rawe, Padstow 1971.
Also Alford, V., *Sword Dance and Drama*, Batsford, London 1962.

5 Stewart, R.J., *The Underworld Initiation*, Aquarian Press, Wellingborough 1985 and 1988.
Also Wimberley, L.C., *Folklore in the English and Scottish Ballads*, Frederick Ungar, New York 1959.

6 Rees, A. and B., *Celtic Heritage*, Thames & Hudson, London 1974.
Also Ross, A., *Pagan Celtic Britain*, Cardinal, London 1974.

7 Bain, G., *Celtic Art*, Reprinted: Constable, London 1977. (Gives technical methods of construction, but no inner significance or background.)

8 Stewart, R.J., *The Waters of the Gap*, Bath City Council 1980. Second edition Ashgrove/Gateway, Bath 1989.
Also Matthews, J. and Stewart, R.J., *Legendary Britain*, Blandford, London 1989.

9 Eliade, M. (trans. W. Trask), *Shamanism, Archaic Techniques of Ecstasy*, Arkana, Harmondsworth 1989.

10 Dillon, M. and Chadwick, N., *The Celtic Realms*, Weidenfeld & Nicolson, New York 1967.
Mac Cana, P., *Celtic Mythology*, Hamlyn, London 1975.

11 Matthews, J. and Stewart, R.J., *Warriors of Arthur*, Blandford Press, London 1987.
Tatlock, J.S.P., *The Legendary History of Britain*, University of California, Berkeley 1950.

12 Julius Caesar, *The Conquest of Gaul* (Gallic Wars, trans. S.A. Handford), Penguin, Harmondsworth 1963.

13 Piggot, S., *The Druids*, Penguin, Harmondsworth 1968.

14 See 6 (Ross) for archaeological information on pagan Anglesey.

15 Matthews, J., *Boadicea*, Firebird Books, Poole 1988.

16 Cunliffe, B., *The Celtic World*, The Bodley Head, London 1979.

17 Stewart, R.J., *Macbeth*, Firebird Books, Poole 1988.

18 Calder, G. (ed.), *The Scholar's Primer*, Edinburgh 1917.
Graves, R., *The White Goddess*, Faber & Faber, London 1975.

19 Bromwich, R., *The Welsh Triads*, Cardiff University Press, 1961.

20 Geoffrey of Monmouth, *History of the Kings of Britain*, various translations.

21 See 5 above.

22 Stewart, R.J., *Cuchulainn*, Firebird Books, Poole 1988.

23 Stewart, R.J.(ed.), *The Book of Merlin*, Blandford Press, London 1987.

24 Stewart, R.J., illustrated by M. Gray, *The Merlin Tarot*, Aquarian Press, Wellingborough 1988. Also 2 and 5 above.

25 See 8 above.

26 Stewart, R.J., *The Mystic Life of Merlin*, Arkana, London 1987. Contains translation and commentary upon the *Vita Merlini* of Geoffrey of Monmouth.

27 Stewart, R.J., *Living Magical Arts*, Blandford Press, Poole 1987.
Also Stewart, R.J., *Advanced Magical Arts*, Element Books, Shaftesbury 1988. Both volumes develop a modern reappraisal of magical traditions and techniques including specific applications of Celtic god and goddess images.

28 See 24 and 26 above.

29 Hull, E. (ed.), *The Cuchulainn Saga*, London 1898.

30 Giraldus Cambrensis, *The History and Topography of Ireland* (various translations, and recently: L. Thorpe, Penguin, Harmondsworth 1982).

31 See 2, 23, 26 above.

32 Fell, B., *America BC, Ancient Settlers in the New World*, Pocket Books, New York 1976.

33 See 8 above.

34 See 24, 26 above.

35 See 11 above.

36 See 17 above.

37 Matarasso, P. (trans.), *The Quest for the Holy Grail*, Penguin, Harmondsworth 1969.

38 See *Legendary Britain*, 8 above, also Matthews, J. and C., *The Aquarian Guide to British and Irish Mythology*, Aquarian Press, Wellingborough 1988.

39 See 32 above.

40 Kirk, R., ed. Sanderson, S., *The Secret Commonwealth*, The Folklore Society, London 1964.
Stewart, R.J., *Robert Kirk: Walker Between the Worlds*, text and commentary upon Kirk's *Secret Commonwealth*, Element Books, Shaftesbury 1990.

41 Yates, F., *The Art of Memory*, Routledge & Kegan Paul, London 1970.

Index of Names and Places

Adam 105, 126
Aeneas 133
Aesculapius 108
Afagddu 88
Amergin 121, 133, 134
Andarta 53
Andraste 29, 80
Angus 135
Annwn 26, 51
Antona 54
Anu 64
Aphrodite 63
Apollo 20, 46, 60, 79, 96, 104, 106–10, 117
Aquae Sulis 18, 21, 41, 52, 54, 63, 92, 96, 98, 108, 109
Arawn 51
Arcturus 52
Ariadne 11, 85, 86, 88
Arianrhod 11, 84, 85, 88
Artemis 53
Arthgen 52
Arthur 11, 26, 44, 52, 79, 106, 109–10, 117, 120–21, 131, 132
Artobranus 52
Artodunum 52
Artogenus 52
Artos 52
Athena 63, 79, 92, 93
Avalon 121

Badhbh 80
Balar 117, 132
Banbha 66, 127, 134
Barinthus 44, 120–22
Bel 45, 98, 104, 108
Belenos 45, 98, 104, 107, 108
Belgae, the 30, 54, 119
Belisima 98
Bellerophon 79
Beltane 62, 108, 132
Bladud 52, 96, 108, 122
Blodeuwedd 63, 83, 85, 116
Boann 110
Bormo 109
Borvo 109
Boudicca 28, 29, 57, 80
Boughton, Rutland 84
Bran 11, 12, 41, 83, 119, 121
Branwen 12, 43, 119
Brid 63, 81
Bride 45, 63, 93–100, 109, 112
Brigantes 96, 98
Brigantia 63, 98
Briggidda 45
Brighid 81, 93–9, 118
Brigit 11, 45, 79, 93–8, 109, 112, 126
Britannia 28
Byanu 64

Caesar 27, 28, 30, 32, 33, 57, 102, 108, 114, 118, 120

Caledon 66
Cambrensis, Giraldus 23, 54
Camlann 120
Caracalla 108
Cassivellaunus 30
Cerne 54, 112
Cernunnos 54, 56, 58, 103, 104, 106, 107, 110, 112, 113, 127
Cerridwen 50, 51, 88, 92
Cessair 127
Christopher, St 124
Cilgwri 109
Citharoedus, Apollo 109
Claudius 28
Cliodna 83
Clyde 28, 121
Columba, St 35
Commodus 28
Cordelia 122
Crearwy 88
Creidhne 118
Cuchulainn 11, 32, 41, 53, 56, 66, 70, 74, 79–82, 114, 116, 124, 134
Culhwch 106, 107, 117, 127

Daedalus 120
Daghdha, the 96, 100, 103, 107, 110, 119, 125, 130, 135
Dalriada 30
Damona 109
Danu 64, 130
Danube, the 26
Davis, F 62
Delphi, oracular shrine at 26, 79, 108
Dian 131, 132
Diana 51
Diancecht 79
Dugal 100
Dyfed 82
Dylan 43, 84

Elbe, the 26
Eochaidh 84, 130
Epona 24, 54, 82
Eriu 66, 134
Esus 34, 40, 54, 104, 105, 112
Etain 54, 83, 84
Etruscans 92
Evrawg 45

Ferdiad 114
Finn 79, 80
Furies 28

Galatia 26
Gildas 37
Giles, J. A. 66, 78, 85
Gofannon 119
Goibhniu 118, 119
Goidels 29
Grannus 108

Graves, Robert 50, 54, 61, 62
Grianainech 108, 123
Guendoloena 63, 113
Guenevere 63, 117
Guest, Lady Charlotte 12, 43, 45, 51, 60, 78, 82, 92, 110
Gwales 41, 42
Gwion 88
Gwydion 51, 84
Gwyn 103, 104
Gwynn 41, 42

Hallstadt 30
Hebrides, the 98
Hecate 51, 92
Heilyn 41, 42
Henvelen 41, 42
Hephaestos 119
Heracles 79
Hercules 122, 123, 124
Hermes 123
Herne 112
Hesiod 79
Hesperides 79
Heywood, Thomas 87
Hibernia 133
Holinshed 122
Holland 115
Hudibras 96
Hull, Eleanor 74, 85, 114

Iberia 133
Iddawc 45
Imbolc 62, 96, 98, 99

Janus 85, 122

Kai 45
Kildare 81, 96
Kilhwch 52, 110
Kirk, Revd Robert 137

Lammas 116
Lancelot 117, 132
Licinia 53
Lleu 100, 116, 117
Llevelys 74, 78, 80
Llew 63, 84, 85, 88
Lludd 74, 80, 117, 118
Llyr 43, 119, 120
Lughnasadh 62, 116
Lugodunum 115, 116
Lugoves 117
Lydney 118
Lyons 45, 115
Lyr 12, 43

Mabinogion, the 11, 36, 41, 43, 45, 51, 52, 54, 58, 60, 63, 64, 74, 78, 80, 81, 82, 84, 85, 98, 100, 105, 106, 109, 110, 113, 116, 119, 127, 135

Mabon 20, 48, 52, 60, 63, 66, 88, 104–9, 110, 124, 125, 131
Macbeth 30
Macha 54, 81
Macleod, Fiona 83, 110
Maia 115
Manannan 43, 120, 121, 122
Manawyddan 41, 42, 120
Maponus 106, 109, 110, 131
Math 51, 63, 84, 116, 119
Matholwch 12
Mathonwy 51, 84, 116, 119
Matres, the 37
Matrona 106
Mercury 95, 112, 114, 115, 116, 117
Merlin 11, 25, 36, 40, 48, 52, 55, 63, 66, 80, 85, 88, 95, 100, 101, 104–7, 113, 117, 118, 121, 122, 124, 127, 128, 131
Midhir 84
Minerva 52, 63, 79, 92, 93, 95, 96, 98, 100
Moccus 51
Moch 51
Modron 64, 66, 106, 109, 110
Mona 28
Monmouth, Geoffrey of 9, 11, 36, 44, 52, 121, 126, 128, 133
Mordred 131
Morgen 63, 120, 121
Morrigan 11, 58, 66, 70, 80, 82, 83, 92, 125, 134

Narberth 82
Navan Fort 81
Nemed 14, 127, 128, 130
Nemetona 128
Nemhain 80
Nennius 106
Neptune 120
Nodons 118, 120, 122
Normandy 86
Nuadha 103, 116–18, 130, 131, 132
Nudd 103, 104, 117, 118

Oenghus 104, 107, 110, 124

Og 110, 135
Ogham 33, 34, 35, 64, 106, 123–4
Oghma 108, 123, 124
Ogmios 107, 122, 123, 124
Olwen 52, 106, 107, 110, 117, 127
Oxford 86, 87, 131

Padstow 12, 50
Pan 113
Parry, J. 101, 113, 120
Partholon 127, 128
Partick, St 54, 135, 136
Pavia 120
Penvro 41, 42
Peredur 45
Perseus 79
Pleiades, the 12, 25, 62, 85
Posidonius 40
Pwyll 51, 82

Rhiannon 41, 54, 81, 82, 83
Rhine, the 26
Rhonabwy 45
Rhydderch 100
Rollright Stones, the 131
Rome 16, 26, 28, 32, 115, 117, 125
Rosamund, Fair 86–8
Rosmerta 115, 116

Sabinilla 53
Scathach 80
Sequana 83
Siberia 107
Sirona 108
Skye 80
Snowdonia 80
Somerset 92, 103
Spain 26, 29, 117, 128, 133, 134
Strabo 40
Sualtam 81
Sucellos 125
Suetonius 28, 41
Sul 21, 41, 92

Sulis 18, 21, 22, 41, 52, 54, 63, 92, 96, 98, 108, 109
Sulis Minerva 41, 92, 108
Switzerland 27, 30

Tacitus 28
Taliesin 41, 88, 95, 121
Tara 84, 116, 130, 134
Taranis 39, 53
Tauros 54
Taurus 62
Ternova 96
Tethra 121, 122
Theseus 79
Thomas 87, 98, 105
Thompson, Aaron 96
Titan 12

Uffington 54
Uisnech 130
Ulster 41, 66, 70, 81, 112, 114, 130, 134

Veneti 30, 32
Venus 63
Vercingetorix 33
Vermont 106
Vortigern 80, 106
Vran 12, 41–3, 119
Vulcan 118

Wales 23, 27, 28, 35, 36, 41, 54, 64, 96, 103, 118, 122, 136
Wayland Smith 119
Westminster 86, 130
Winchester 66
Windsor 112
Woodstock 86, 106

Yates, F. 33
Ynawc 41
York 34

Zeus 39, 79

General Index

Alphabet, sacred 34, 48, 123, 124
Altar(s) 14, 28, 34, 40, 104
America, Celts in 25, 34, 40, 137
Ancestors, divine nature of 18, 43, 44, 48, 102, 112, 126, 133, 135
Animals, religious and magical 13, 20, 34, 37, 48, 50, 51, 54–8, 59, 60, 78, 88, 99, 104, 106, 107, 109, 112, 113, 115, 124, 127
Animism 23
Apple, sacred 83, 120, 121
Archaeology 9, 10, 19, 22
Arming, ritual function of 88
Armour 70, 80, 81, 114

Bards 9, 35, 44, 51, 101, 109, 117
Bear 21, 33, 41, 48, 52, 53, 66, 108, 114, 134
Beauty 46, 82, 84, 87, 110, 120, 121, 125, 136
Buddhism 20
Birds 40, 41, 54, 82, 83, 109
Birth 50, 51, 62, 81, 84, 88, 98, 107
Boar 48, 50, 51, 52, 79, 107, 109, 134
Boat 39, 121, 128
Brothers, motif and myth of 39, 40, 60, 85, 105, 117, 118,
Bull 40, 48, 53, 54, 104

Calendars 45, 58
Cat 50, 56
Cattle 21, 32, 66, 70, 74, 79, 80, 121, 122, 132
Cauldron sacred 26, 78, 88, 92, 109, 112, 119, 125, 130, 131
Cave(s) 15, 23, 38
Ceremonies 12, 41, 53, 92, 96, 99, 108, 116
Chariot 32, 70, 74, 85, 108
Chess 84, 116
Christ, Celtic 21, 100, 104, 105, 107, 124
Christianity 11, 19, 78, 81, 85, 92, 101, 102, 104, 105, 113, 126
Club 59, 60, 122, 125
Cock 115
Cockerel 99
Cosmology 9, 10, 11, 29, 36, 48, 52, 95, 109, 113, 118, 128, 130, 133
Cow 70, 74, 96, 109
Cowherds 58
Cranes 54, 104
Creation 9, 53, 85, 88, 103, 104, 106, 109, 118, 119, 124, 126, 127, 128, 130, 134
Crone 51, 62, 63, 82, 88
Crow 48, 80
Cup 131
Cupbearer 116, 132

Death 11, 12, 38, 41, 51, 52, 56, 58, 62, 66, 74, 80, 81, 84, 85, 87, 88, 92, 100, 101, 105, 107, 108, 110, 113, 116, 119, 121, 122, 125, 128, 134, 135
Decapitation 41
Deer 58, 113
Divination 95

Dragons 60, 74, 78–80, 117
Dreams 18
Dream-women 82
Druidesses 28
Druidism 125
Druids 14, 23, 28, 33, 38, 53, 54, 81, 104, 115, 128, 132
Duck, sacred 83

Eagle 110, 127
Earth 37, 39, 64, 66, 78, 79, 112, 115, 118, 131, 134, 135
East 25, 26, 96, 101, 114, 130
Elements, the 12, 19, 20, 29, 30, 35, 50, 54, 61, 64, 79, 100, 102, 103, 108, 118, 119, 128, 131, 132
Empire, Roman 21, 26–7, 28, 51

Fairies, Celtic traditions of 21, 43, 135–7
Father, divine 9, 39, 86, 103, 110, 116, 125, 131
Feast 42, 50, 96, 98, 119, 125, 128
Ferryman, divine 121, 122
Fertility 24, 50, 54, 58, 62, 74, 81, 82, 99, 112, 125, 132
Festivals 25, 62, 81
Fire 32, 45, 79, 80, 81, 96, 98, 100, 101, 112, 118, 131, 132, 134
Folklore 9, 11, 15, 16, 33, 39, 40, 41, 45, 56, 78, 80, 92, 98, 118, 122
Food 42, 50, 66, 98, 110, 125
Forest 12, 38, 66, 112, 121
Fortnight, lunar period of 58
Fosterage 98
Foster-mother 92, 100
Fruit 19, 53, 63, 121

Giant(s) 12, 25, 39, 52, 66, 79, 87, 109, 113, 119
Goats 55, 125
God-child 48, 52
God-forms 22
God-king 96, 119
God-names 38
Guardian, the divine 12, 41, 52, 107, 117
Guardianship 40, 107
Gündestrup Cauldron, the 29, 112, 119

Hag 58
Hair 28, 100, 109
Haruspex 21
Harvest 116, 121, 132
Hawk 127, 134
Hazel 39
Hazelwood 70
Head, sacred 41–3, 45, 54, 56, 74, 85, 105, 108, 114, 132
Herd 51, 52, 55, 113
Herdsman 113
Heroes 9, 11, 20, 26, 41, 48, 50, 52, 63, 78, 79, 80, 94, 107, 109, 125
Hobby-horses 56

Hog 114
Horse 12, 24, 45, 48, 50, 54, 59, 70, 74, 79, 82, 83, 84, 101, 113, 119
Hound 39, 41, 56, 57, 114
Hunt, the 51, 54, 79, 103, 107, 109
Hurling 33

Idols 21
Indo-Europeans, the 25, 96
Inspiration 16, 18, 38, 45, 88, 95, 96, 99, 118, 122
Invasions 13, 14, 29, 30, 61, 122, 126–33
Islands 66, 92, 98, 103

Javelins 33

King 11, 12, 23, 30, 33, 44, 45, 51, 52, 54, 66, 74, 78, 80, 81, 84, 86, 87, 88, 100, 106, 107, 108, 109, 116, 117, 118, 120, 121, 122, 130, 131, 132, 135
Kingship 9, 15, 30, 52, 54, 80, 84, 88, 94, 100, 101, 104, 117, 118, 130, 131, 132, 134

Labyrinth 86, 88
Lakes 12, 40, 128, 132, 134
Lambs 121
Lammas, feast of 116
Lance, sacred 125
Legionaries, Roman 28

Magic 9, 10, 12, 18, 20, 24, 26, 30, 36, 43, 50, 54, 55, 74, 82, 85, 118, 119, 121, 125, 130, 132, 133, 136
Magicians 20, 48, 50
Maiden, goddess as 58, 62, 63, 66, 80, 82, 83, 84, 85, 96, 100, 113, 116
Mare 23, 39, 54
Mating, ritual 99, 125
Matres, the 37
Mayday 62
Metaphysics 12, 50, 102, 128
Milk 125, 128, 132
Mistletoe 38, 39
Moon, the 40, 44–6, 58, 85, 100, 108, 121
Mother, goddesses as 9, 23, 37, 39, 40, 50, 58, 60–64, 81, 84, 86, 88, 92, 98, 100, 104, 105, 106, 108, 109, 110, 131
Mothers, the 107
Mounds, ancient 15, 135, 136
Music 107, 109, 121

Navigation 44
Necromancy 52, 96
Night 33, 42, 45, 59, 62, 79, 100
North 28, 35, 40, 52, 66, 70, 85, 106, 109, 114, 128, 130
November 25, 62, 125, 128

Oak 32, 38, 39, 109
Oars 32

Oats 125
Ocean 42, 79, 120
Otherworld, the 15, 38, 40, 50, 52, 55, 70, 82, 83, 84, 119, 120, 121, 122, 124, 128, 130, 136
Ousel 109
Owl 83, 109
Oxen 51, 66

Pagan(ism) 11, 12, 13, 18–23, 35–7, 40, 41, 43, 45, 53, 54, 55, 58, 61, 62, 78, 86, 88, 92, 96, 98, 99, 100, 101, 105, 106, 110, 117, 118, 125, 126, 137
Paradise 82, 121, 122
Picts 30
Pigs 51, 52, 78, 125
Planets 62, 128
Plants 15, 34, 37, 48, 56
Poems 25, 34, 35, 36
Poetry 9, 23, 82, 87, 95, 96, 106, 114, 123, 125, 128, 132
Poets 19, 35, 38, 88, 107, 113, 136
Porridge 125
Priestess(es) 63, 120
Priesthood 38
Priests 128
Primitivism 23
Primogeniture 57, 132
Prophecies 11, 25, 36, 41, 63, 66, 80, 85, 88, 106, 113, 117, 118, 122, 128
Prophecy 41, 51, 92, 99, 106, 107, 118
Prophet(s) 36, 38, 52, 80, 95, 101, 107
Psychology 13, 102
Psychopomp 52, 124
Python 108

Queen, ancient role of 28, 54, 57, 63, 66, 80, 83–7, 96, 99, 100, 118, 124

Ram 48, 112, 115
Raven 80, 83
Religion 9, 10, 11, 12, 14, 15, 18, 20, 21, 22, 23, 25, 26, 28, 30, 33, 35–8, 40, 48, 50, 54, 57, 58, 61, 64, 66, 74, 78, 92, 100, 102, 106, 117, 126, 128, 132, 133, 137
Ritual 12, 23, 40, 50, 53–5, 64, 81, 99, 100, 105, 107, 109, 112–13, 115, 116, 125, 126
River(s) 15, 26, 28, 37, 40, 43, 45, 63, 66, 83, 100, 101, 110, 122, 124, 125, 128, 132
Roman(s) 10, 13, 14, 16, 18, 19, 20, 21, 22, 28, 30, 32–5, 37, 41, 46, 51, 52, 57, 63, 80, 92, 95, 96, 102, 103, 104, 106, 108, 114, 115, 120, 126

Saints 20, 40, 41, 126
Salmon 110, 121, 127, 134
Samhain 62, 125, 128
Sanctuary 28, 63, 81, 96
Sapling 109
Satire 132
Satirist 74
Saxons 80, 119
Scone, sacred centre of 130
Scots, the 9, 29, 36, 57, 127
Sea 12, 28, 39, 42, 43, 44, 66, 83, 100, 103, 120, 121, 122, 134

Seasons 39, 48, 61, 88
Sea-deities 121
Seer(s) 36, 107
Seership 53
Serpents 54, 56, 60, 78, 79, 80, 99, 100, 112, 113
Sexuality 11, 58, 74, 92, 99, 112, 125
Shaman 107, 127
Shamanism 20
Shape-changing 82, 92, 127
Sheep 45, 113, 125
She-goats 113
Shield 114, 131
Shipbuilding 30
Ships 12, 30, 52, 120
Shoemakers, legendary 117
Shoe-making, skill of 116
Shrines 14, 15, 21, 23, 43, 108
Sidh, people of the 15, 134–7; *see also* Fairies, Celtic traditions of
Singing 41, 74, 83
Sisters, divine 63, 79, 96, 120, 121
Sister-son 57
Skills, Celtic emphasis upon 28, 30, 32, 35, 45, 80, 93, 96, 114, 116, 117, 119, 121, 122, 126, 128, 132
Skulls 41
Sky 25, 39, 40, 60, 108
Smith 118, 119, 131, 132
Smithcraft 96, 118
Son, divine 9, 29, 39, 40–2, 45, 51, 52, 58, 60, 66, 81, 83, 84, 86, 88, 96, 98, 100, 102, 104, 105, 106, 108, 109, 110, 119, 120, 122, 127
Soul(s) 84, 99, 102, 104, 105, 124, 133
Sovereign 9, 120
Sovereignty, goddesses of 11, 23, 66, 84, 88, 95, 100, 116, 117, 118, 127, 132, 134, 137
Sow 50, 88
Spear 74, 114, 117, 125, 130, 131, 134
Spider 98
Spiral 79
Spiralled 48
Spring 12, 14, 23, 66, 96, 98, 99, 108
Springs, sacred, 15, 18, 22, 23, 37, 38, 40, 41, 52, 66, 98, 107–10, 132
Stag 48, 54, 55, 60, 101, 109, 112, 113, 134
Stars 11, 12, 25, 26, 39, 40, 44, 60, 62, 64, 85, 109, 110, 120, 121, 128
Statuary 18
Statues 14, 114
Statuettes 53
Stones, sacred and standing 14, 15, 32, 34, 66, 105, 114, 123, 130, 131
Story-cycles 44
Story-telling 13, 14, 101, 109
Sun, divinity or worship of 20, 40, 44–6, 58, 62, 96, 100, 108, 121, 122, 134
Superstition 23, 33, 37, 45, 118
Swans 84
Swine 51, 52
Swineherds 12
Sword 23, 39, 85, 114, 130, 131

Taboo(s) 56, 57
Tales, mythology preserved in oral 11, 12, 35,
36, 40, 52, 58, 63, 64, 79, 80, 100, 102, 115, 117, 118, 122, 132
Tanist 117
Tarot, mythic images within 101, 113, 131
Temples 14, 16, 21, 23, 34, 96, 102, 130
Therapy 41, 45, 52, 79, 96, 107, 109, 118, 121
Totem(s) 20, 29, 41, 48, 50, 52, 54, 56, 57, 79, 83, 88, 96, 99, 104, 109, 112, 115, 118, 127
Totemism 56, 57
Tradition 9–20, 29, 32, 38, 39, 40, 44, 50, 52, 54, 55, 57, 58, 62, 63, 66, 80, 83, 85, 86, 88, 92, 95, 96, 98, 101, 102–5, 107, 108, 109, 112, 113, 117, 119, 120, 121, 122, 125, 126, 127, 128, 130, 131, 132, 133, 134, 135, 136
Tree(s) 12, 14, 15, 34, 38, 39, 40, 45, 48, 54, 83, 100, 101, 104, 105, 109, 120, 121, 124, 128
Triads, poetic and bardic 34, 106, 107

UnderWorld, the sacred 11, 15, 26, 30, 37, 38, 40, 41, 50, 51, 52, 54, 88, 92, 94, 99, 100, 102–4, 106, 108, 109, 112, 118, 119, 122, 128, 131, 132, 134, 135

Verse(s) 14, 98, 121, 124, 133
Virginity 62, 85
Virgins 99, 105
Visualization 20
Visualized 121
Vita Merlini, the 44, 52, 55, 63, 95, 100–1, 103, 106–7, 113, 119, 120, 121, 127, 128

Warrior(s) 26, 28, 32, 57, 60, 63, 70, 79, 80, 84, 106, 109, 116, 119, 130, 132, 133
Washer, goddess as 80
Washing, symbolism of 80, 81, 125
Water 12, 18, 21, 28, 33, 40, 41, 43, 66, 80, 96, 98, 100, 101, 108, 118, 131
Waves 26, 30, 121, 126, 127
Weapons 70, 114, 119, 121, 132
Weaver, goddess as 85, 98
Wells 23, 38, 40, 41, 43, 52, 132
West, the 12, 18, 26, 29, 64, 70, 96, 103, 104, 114, 130, 132
Westminster 86, 130
Wheel(s) 11, 32, 39, 61, 70, 74, 85, 88, 113
Winter 12, 61
Witchcraft 57
Wolf 48
Womb 108, 121
Woods 12, 59, 66, 110, 113, 120, 121, 123
Woodland 112
Woodward 59
Worlds 40, 46, 50, 96, 104, 108, 109, 119, 124, 128, 131, 133, 137
Worship 10, 11, 14, 16, 19, 20, 21, 23, 24, 30, 37, 38, 41, 44, 45, 46, 48, 50, 54, 64, 92, 98, 99, 102, 108, 112, 136
Wound 87, 100, 120, 121
Wounded 41, 44, 83, 100, 116, 117, 120, 121

Yew 105
Youth 88, 100, 107, 109
Youthful 80, 106, 107, 109, 115, 131, 135

Zodiac 85